The Power

~

A Call To Mediumship

Reverend Nicole Powell

For privacy reasons, some names may have been changed. Where real people have been included, their permission has been granted. This book includes memories, from my perspective, and I have tried to represent events as faithfully as possible.

First paperback edition May 2024

Book cover photography by Brandy-Lee Planiden

Cover designed by Shannon-Leanne Du Plessis

Dedication

This book is dedicated to my mom and dad. Mom for teaching me to be loving and owning my power. For my dad for teaching me discernment and self-discipline. Together, you have taught me to be strong and to honour myself. Thank you.

Table Of Contents

Preface

This book is written from my own knowledge and personal experience. I have been in private practice as a healer and tarot reader since 2012 and have been in full-time private practice with evidential mediumship since 2015. My day-in and day-out experience working with clients and communing with the spirit world has led me to this wealth of knowledge about spirit communication and the other side. I have no desire to convert you but to share my experience since it all began. I will share my awakening to spirituality, personal stories, and understanding of how communing with spirits from the other side works. Take what you need and leave the rest.

I choose to share my knowledge for inspiration and teaching purposes. All situations sharing stories with clients are dubbed with pseudonyms to protect the client's privacy, as well as situations from long ago not to be obvious who the people involved may be. All other names sharing personal stories have been given with permission from my friends.

I have gathered these stories since the beginning and have been an avid daily journaler since I was seven. Most of these stories written in such detail are because of journal entries and personal Facebook posts on my business page (my personal experiences, not client stories) that have been written with the knowledge that these stories would be shared again. This is to bring accuracy and timelines to this book. They have also been shared in my inspired speaking at Spiritualist Churches and with my students in mediumship circle.

I weave my personal experiences with teachable moments of wisdom that will help you here and in the future. Sharing honest experiences and life stories accurately is important to me, and I have my family and friends to hold me accountable. When I share personal encounters and stories of spirit, more magic can happen. My clients, students and spiritual friends have asked me to write this book as I have too many "Nicole stories" not to share. They also feel that I need to be honest about the day-in and day-out of being a spiritual medium.

Dubbed pseudo names in this book to protect privacy: Steve, Jean Pierre, Michelle, Brad, Cait, Lindsay, Jake, Julie, Eric, Sandy, Cindy, Craig, Darlene

First Nations Cowichan elder Lana Ryan gave full permission for this book to include information about the native language and some cultural traditions in the Cowichan Valley for teaching purposes.

Editor's Note By Katie Oman

In 2010, I had my spiritual awakening after the sudden and tragic death of my grandparents from a house fire. The trauma cracked me open and made me question so many things –who I am, why I'm here, and what I want to do. Until that point in my life, I had been like an oarless boat on a turbulent ocean, without a map, compass or sail. I had no real sense of direction and allowed the waves of life to take me where they wished to.

A few months later, I met a friend of my mum's called Barbara, who was a psychic medium. The very first words out of her mouth when she met me weren't *"Hello"* or *"Nice to meet you."* No, her words upon meeting me were, *"You can do what I can do, you know."* I was stunned. It was never something I had considered for myself. Oh, I knew I was different from the people around me. I am a highly sensitive, empathic and intuitive person in many ways, but I was consistently told that this wasn't something to be celebrated in life. Instead, I was constantly made to feel that I was a problem that didn't fit in and needed to be solved.

Over the next few months, Barbara helped me to connect to my innate abilities. I was a natural with both the tarot and oracle cards, and so divination was something I developed.

As mentioned, though, Barbara was a medium, and she sought to help me tap into this ability, too. The problem was that my highly sensitive nature was terrified! I was inherently scared of what might come through – hardly a good energy to be trying to work with! You have probably heard of the Law of Attraction, where you draw to you that which you consistently focus on. Sure enough, I began to have paranormal experiences that only served to confirm my fears, for example, the time when I visited The Shakespeare Experience in Stratford-Upon-Avon and saw the dismembered head of a man who was growling at me. Later on, when I described him, I was told that he was a notorious man who had raped and murdered a lot of women! So, as you can imagine, I quickly accepted the fact that mediumship wasn't for me. Instead, I chose to work with the angelic realms, which felt safer and lighter in every sense.

How I wish *The Power: A Call to Mediumship* were around back then! I know without a doubt that it would've helped me to alleviate some of the fears that were clouding my mind, as well as potentially helping me connect to that psychic ability within myself. Nicole not only provides detailed wisdom and knowledge about this topic that is born from her own experiences, but she does so in a warm and inviting manner. You feel as though you are being supported by a nurturing guide who understands you. With each chapter, you truly feel like you are being led on a journey back to yourself to explore the potential of all you are. Nicole's kindness of spirit and warm humour radiate off each page, with not a smidge of doubt or fear to be found.

Being Nicole's book coach and editor for *The Power: A Call to Mediumship* has been both a privilege and an honour. Together, Nicole and I have dived deep into her story so far to help bring it to the pages of this book. I know you will find it as fascinating and heartwarming as I do. Reading this book, it becomes abundantly clear that mediumship isn't some scary, demon-filled movie that'll have you diving under the covers. In truth, it's a beautiful service that connects people to their loved ones in spirit in the most heart-centred way possible. To understand that now feels like the most blessed gift.

Katie Oman is a book coach, author and women's empowerment coach. To find out more, go to https://www.katieoman.co.uk.

Opening

"Not all those who wander are lost." - J. R. R. Tolkien

Each person I meet comes to mediumship in their own way - from the death of a loved one, a traumatic event that activated it, curiosity, or being born with it (hereditary) and wanting to know how to turn it off or control it.

How you find your way to mediumship is unique to you. The most important thing is realising that you have been led by a power greater than yourself. It brought you to this place of deep inquiry to discover what lies within and to build a relationship with the divine. Your path to mediumship will be your own, as no one else walks in your shoes. It will be an adventure of a lifetime.

Let me share a bit about how I got started….

Introduction

~

The Calling

"The moment of surrender is not when life is over. It's when it begins." - Marianne Williamson, *A Return To Love*

July 2007

I was lying on my back on the hospital bed, staring up at the bright neon lights of the ceiling. I was terrified to move as the sharp stomach pain was unbearable. At 7am I was alone in the empty, sterile emergency room in a small-town hospital, in BC, Canada. My boyfriend of five months dropped me off at the curb, having listened to me complain about my stomach for three weeks. He was feeling helpless and frustrated that he couldn't do anything about it and he hoped I'd find answers from the doctors this time. It was my third time in an emergency that week, not to mention the two visits to the walk-in clinic, and calling the nurses' hotline the night before.

I had spent the night alone in my apartment, lying on my bathroom floor, unable to move. I had taken multiple heavy-duty pain meds with codeine. My stomach was inflated like a balloon, and I had a hot water bottle lying over me.

I was surprised I had woken up that morning as I thought for sure there was no way I could live through another night experiencing the sharp stabbing pains. I had been missing work almost every day for nearly two weeks without any answers about what was happening to me. I had sharp lower abdominal pain that was so excruciating that I'd cry or feel faint if I moved too quickly. I had black circles under my eyes; my skin was white as a ghost; I was the thinnest I had ever been (after continuous dieting that year, losing 30 pounds), and I felt as if I was going in and out of consciousness.

I couldn't understand why I wasn't receiving any help from the doctors when I had gone in saying I was in pain. It was like wherever I went or whoever I asked help from was in a trance and saw right through me. Never once was a blood test done, an X-ray or ultrasound conducted. Each time, they asked questions to determine if I was simply seeking out some kind of narcotics as if I was an addict and wondering if I had been using (I had never done drugs in my life. Well, okay, I had a phase where I smoked some pot in high school, but nothing else). Looking in the mirror, I could see why they would have thought that. I didn't look like a 22-year-old woman anymore, I looked rough. They also told me I probably had an STD and to call my GP for an exam. I was sent home with more pain meds, told to take them every 4-6 hours, and that in a few days it should work itself out.

But that morning was different from the days in the previous weeks. I felt so close to death. The veil was so thin, and it felt like I was dipping in and out of this world. After waking up from being blacked out on the bathroom floor, I couldn't bear another moment of living like this. I had already lost two very close friends my age to misdiagnoses in the past three years, and I didn't need to be another statistic of doctors over-seeing young adult women only to die suddenly of untreated medical conditions that could be treated.

As I lay in the hospital bed waiting, I was aware the doctor and nurses were having a meeting about me in this small-town hospital. They didn't understand why I was there again. As the tears poured down my face, feeling completely misunderstood and dismissed, listening to the slight mumblings from the other room, I prayed and asked the Creator for help.

I spoke words of desperation under my breath, and I noticed from the corner of my eye a bright white light starting to glow on the right side of the room. This light grew brighter as it started to shape like a human figure. It began to move towards me and came close up to my face. I thought I was losing any sense of reality now. I was exhausted, with the fear of death becoming more and more apparent. I cried out loud, thinking this was an Angel of Death coming to get me to take me home.

"I'm not ready!" I exclaimed as the tears dripped down my face.

The figure stood there as a bright light. Now I was able to see her face. She had a translucent look about her and porcelain skin. She was dressed in a long white gown and was beautiful. I was glowing in her presence. I could feel she was gentle and kind, swaying around me, stopping on the right side of my face.

"You have a choice," she said to me in a soft voice.

"I don't want to go with you" I whispered. *"You have already taken two of my close friends. I can't let you do this to my family, not after what I saw you do to theirs."*

I was whimpering now, a deep sorrow overcoming me. I was aware of what grief did to people and how it changed those they loved and their lives. I wasn't willing to do that to my family, not now.

"If you do not want to come with me, then you will have to do this work."

I looked at her, confused. *"What work?"* I whispered back to her.

She giggled. *"Don't worry, we'll show you."* And then, just as quickly as she had appeared, she faded into the light.

A brief moment after she left, I barely had a minute to process what had happened, and the doctor walked back into the room. This was the first time this particular doctor had seen me. I recognised him from the hair salon I had worked in as a hairstylist, and I knew he had recognised me too. In his thick South African accent, he enquired, *"Nicole, has anyone taken your blood work in these past couple of weeks?"*

"No" I replied. I smiled, appreciating that this was the first time a doctor had even considered doing a test to find out what was happening beneath the surface. The closest I got before was another walk-in clinic prescribing a course of antibiotics, thinking it could have been my kidneys, but no further blood work had been taken.

"Alright," he replied, *"Let's start with that."*

Moments later, a nurse showed up with lab work, and then I was carted for an X-ray. Starting to be treated like a patient, I told her, *"Oh, this is different, I've never been wheeled in a wheelchair before."*

She rolled her eyes and snickered. *"If you are going to come to the emergency, we will have to treat you like this is an emergency."* She said back to me. I could tell it was the end of her night shift, and I tried not to take what she said personally.

Within the hour, an ambulance showed up and transferred me onto the stretcher. I was sent to St Paul's Hospital in the next major city, Vancouver, BC. I had initially intended to go there from Squamish, but a rock landslide had cut off the road. As it turns out, the highway had been cleared just before the ambulance took me to Vancouver.

My appendix had ruptured in 2 places, it was leaking septicaemia into my abdomen, and I needed emergency surgery and treatment fast.

****

May 2008

The year that followed involved a lot of physical pain, suffering and surgical trauma. I was officially home and away from hospitals. That last few months, I was in and out of the hospital and doctor's appointments, having various procedures done and was now considered healed from my experience and on the road to recovery.

But I was far from even remotely healed. I was raw, in physical and emotional pain, uncomfortable in my body and feeling completely removed from my old life. My previous life of showing up to work, doing my 9-5 job, keeping a smile on my face while I did hairdressing and trying to move forward was the farthest thing from being real I could possibly think of.

I was longing for something more, and I felt with my brush with death that I was given an opportunity to expand from my old ways of life. Nothing was wrong with my life, but I felt like something was off with me if I stayed where I was. I did enjoy what I did for a living. I had good friends, I was in a network and community of like-minded people. But there was a yearning in my soul that felt dislocated from the whole.

I also felt like I was living outside of my body. I had spent months taking pain medication and antibiotics, having various procedures to vacuum and drain the septicemia out of my system. I experienced invasive and painful interventions on my organs, having my appendix removed and wearing a drain bag, which was removing various green fluids from my abdomen. My body felt violated, as if I was at war with it, resulting in anxiety and nightmares.

When I looked in the mirror at work in the hair salon, I looked empty. There was a huge void within me. I had to trust I was being led to the next step of my life. I had to trust that there was a better life for me if I stayed open and let myself be led.

I told my mom that I felt like I was being guided to new work and I had outgrown my work life but couldn't quite figure out what I was supposed to do. She told me there was an article in the newspaper about Sylvia Brown, a Psychic Medium, coming to Victoria, BC, for Mother's Day. She was going to be doing an evening event, and she would be doing live audience readings. She said if I came home for the weekend, she'd love for us to go together. This was a great way to spend Mother's Day weekend with my mom.

"You never know," my mom said, *"you might just end up with a reading."*

A huge smile filled my face, and I knew with every fibre in my being that I would be invited up on stage to get a reading from her.

The night came quickly, and we arrived early, entering the auditorium that could fit close to 800 people. The usher gave us each a red 50/50 ticket and told us that if our number was called, we could come down to the front stage and ask Sylvia 1 question. I took my ticket and rubbed it for good luck. I closed my eyes and visualised my number being called.

As the night progressed and Sylvia came out talking about her usual end of days and what to expect on the other side, the host came up and started calling out the numbers. I held my ticket close, waiting for my numbers to be called. He spoke for a good few minutes, calling out approximately 20-30 numbers, but not once were my numbers called. I was in shock, and I could not believe I wouldn't get to ask Sylvia a question. I swore I was guided here, and that all felt too synchronistic. I just stared at my ticket in disbelief that it wasn't called.

Suddenly, a woman sitting directly behind me tapped me on the shoulder. I reluctantly turned around, breaking my stare of disbelief that I wasn't called. She was an older woman, probably in her 80s, and she looked straight at me with the most sincere blue eyes and an open heart. She handed me her ticket and said, *"You look like you need this more than I do."* She passed me her ticket and saw the complete joy that filled my heart. I saw her eyes get glossy and red. I was so incredibly grateful for her, and I thanked her profusely that she gave me this gift.

I marched down to the front of the stage. As the usher passed me the microphone, I looked at Sylvia and said to her. *"I need your help. I am 23 and feel like I am supposed to be on a different path than the one I am on. What direction would be my highest and best intention to walk down for my future?"*

Sylvia barely skipped a beat. She looked at me, but beyond me into my aura, and shouted back in her deep voice, *"You're a healer, dear."* Then, cued the host to pass the mic to the next person in line.

I walked back to my chair on the second balcony, totally confused. *"What was a healer?"* I thought to myself. Quiet for the rest of the evening, I went home and opened my parent's Windows desktop computer. I typed in the Google search *HEALER*, wondering what the heck that was and how to get on the path to be one.

****

About a month later, my boss, Marian, told me, *"Nicole, have you tried energy healing? I just had one, and you have been through a lot. Maybe you need your energy rebalanced after everything you've gone through this past year. Maybe someone could give you a reset."*

It piqued my interest. Until then, I had never really heard of energy healing or Reiki, but without knowing what it was, I knew I needed it. Besides, it had the word healing, so I paid more attention. I found a local healer in Squamish named Erica Otto, who was more than willing to give me healing and teach me how to do Reiki Levels 1 and 2.

My first session was an unforgettable spiritual experience. I was put right back into my body, and the excess energy was swept off my energy field. I felt as though fractals of my soul came back to me after feeling as if I was living outside of myself in a dream for almost a year. That first healing was a turning point for the direction in which I wanted to take my health and future. So much so that, within a few weeks of that first healing, I signed up for a 3-year program at Langara College in Vancouver, BC, studying Integrative Energy Healing. I wanted to know everything I could possibly learn about healing work. I wanted to be more in tune with my body and trust its wisdom, which always knows what I need. I had a choice in the matter to heal my life. There was more to life than managing pain, taking various pills to numb out and handing over all my power to a medical team. I was allowed to speak up, I didn't have to stay quiet and assume others knew how to heal me.

When I stepped into the paradigm of looking at the role I played in my own suffering, my world changed in an instant.

Energy healing taught me that I was responsible for my life, that a power greater than me could restore me to sanity if I let it in, and that there was more to life than managing pain and running from it. If I felt my feelings, used my voice, and allowed the stuck energy to move, I could step on a path to a new life. But I had to be willing and vulnerable to look at those parts of myself that maybe I wasn't ready to see. When I could move those energetic cobwebs away, there was buried treasure within. There were gifts waiting to be claimed that were so stuffed down that I didn't even know they existed.

But mainly, I had to face my grief. There was so much grief within me.

Chapter 1: Awakening

~

Where Grief Met Me

"You can't go back and change the beginning, but you can start where you are and change the ending." - CS Lewis.

February, 1995

I was ten years old when I had my first experience with death. My next-door neighbour Steve. He was my favourite babysitter and someone I saw most days. He and his younger brother were always welcome to come and go at our house, as my older brother Michael was a close friend to both of them. At 14 years of age, Steve took his own life. He jumped off the back of a cruise ship on a family vacation in Florida, leaving a suicide note and shoes on the back of the ship deck. His body was never found, and his mom, dad and brother were devastated. There was just no explanation for what he had done, with no lead-up or depression that anyone was aware of. Anyone in his life would have thought he was a happy teenage boy.

We were on a family vacation in Tacoma, Seattle, when it happened early in the new year while my brother was in a hockey tournament. We were staying at the Embassy Suites Hotel when my mom called my brother and I into the hotel room that evening after talking to my grandmother on the phone. She was shaking, sobbing and trying to catch her breath. My dad was quiet, sitting on the edge of the bed with his head down. They tried to explain to us in a matter of a few broken words that Steve was gone, and it was on the news.

"Gone where?" I asked.

"Nicole", my mom said softly, *"Steve died."*

"I don't get it," I replied, my mind numb in the shock of what I was hearing. *"How? What? What do you mean, he chose to die?"*

Up until that point in my life, I had never thought about death before. I had never questioned my life, nor had I lost anyone I loved. I had never considered what happened to people when they were no longer here. It just hadn't sunken in for me yet, and I had never even heard about death being something that people could choose to do, that that was even an option. Why would Steve want to leave this world? Did he know where he was going?

Nothing was ever the same after that day. Our playful street seemed even more quiet. Grief filled the air, and questions of the afterlife filled my mind and thoughts. I couldn't understand why Steve had done it. He was at our house the day before he left for his family vacation on a cruise. We were listening to his new Eagles CD he was given for Christmas. We hung out with my family in the living room, talking, laughing and listening to music like nothing was wrong. He didn't seem sad; I remember him smiling. I remember when Steve left the house that day. He walked down the front stairs of our home, and I followed behind him. I was always curious and quite observant of him. He walked across the yard towards his house, and halfway across the lawn, he looked back at me and held a gaze for a few seconds. I realise now that it was as if he was looking back just one last time. I remember the image of him looking back and locking eyes with me. At the moment, it was nothing, but in my soul, it was everything. A smile filled my face. As a 10-year-old, I looked up to him, for Steve was the coolest guy in the world.

I was no longer a stranger to the concept of death, and over the next nine years, more people I loved died. First, my grandfather on my mother's side at age 13 (he was one of my favourite people), then my grandfather on my father's side when I was 17, and then two of my best friends at 19. Mary, my kindred spirit, passed from a misdiagnosed meningitis; you'll hear more about that in the next section. Then there was Crista (one of my great friends from high school), who died three months after Mary died of leukemia she didn't know she had. Grief, numbness, and sorrow were all around me, and it affected me mentally. I felt out of control. The people I loved seemed to be passing away. I believe the prolonged stress is what made me so physically sick to my stomach when I was 22, but also that it was a part of my journey to experience loss. On a higher level, I chose to look for meaning and purpose in my life because of it. I became hyper-aware that life was not something I could ever take for granted.

Mary

"The wound is a place where light enters you." - Rumi

December 23rd, 2004

      I was getting ready for one of my last workdays before the holidays. I finished my hair and put on my lip gloss before the phone rang. I jumped to grab it in my mom and dad's room on the corded phone landline. I had been using their bathroom to curl my hair with the curling iron.

As I jumped onto the phone, I was only half there as I was already thinking about who my first haircut of the day would be. My best friend Mary's older brother called me first thing in the morning. I thought it was odd. Especially since I didn't know he would have my phone number, nor did I really have a relationship with him.

"Hi Nicole, it's Mary's brother," he said to me in a matter-of-fact way. *"I've called to let you know that Mary didn't make it. She was in the hospital last night. She had meningitis."*

"Huh?" I replied.

As the phone froze in my hand, I began to shake from the inside of my being. This throbbing pain started creeping into my throat suddenly as I noticed my breath begin to shorten, lightness began to fill my head, and black spots started to fill the space before me.

I didn't understand. I had one million questions, yet I had none. I saw Mary two days ago in town. She worked as a salesperson selling soap and make-up at The Bay Centre's Body Shop in Victoria, BC.

Mary was colourful, bright blue-eyed, blonde, free-spirited and theatrical. People thought she was my sister. She worked for my mother, as my mom was the store manager. Mary was more than just a friend. She was my soul sister, kindred spirit, sister from another mother, chosen adopted family, neighbourhood friend, best friend in high school, and someone I adored more than most people I knew in my life. My mom and dad even had a permanent bed set up for her in my bedroom so Mary could stay whenever she liked. I could stay at her house too whenever I wanted. Sometimes, even late at night, she would walk over, or I would walk over to her house to have a friend nearby. Just knowing she was there made life better. We had a way of enhancing each other. Since we had graduated high school, we were being stretched to grow up and find our way in life. But we bonded more than ever as we grew into our new adult selves at 19.

"What do you mean died?" I said to him over the phone. I started to feel stupid as I didn't even know she was sick.

"She had meningitis. She didn't make it." He spoke quietly and sternly. And then he said he had to go, but that their mother would like to see me. He hung up the phone.

I stared blankly at the wall with my mouth agape and couldn't move. My body was paralysed and frozen, and I just sat there as time and space stood still. I felt myself dip in and out of reality as the wall before me seemed to move as I blinked my eyes. I was lightheaded, not really present, and afraid to move because I wasn't ready to let things set in. At that moment, the world stood still, tipped on its atlas, and I was trying to find a moment to grasp there was a way up.

I picked up the phone again and called my work, my voice shaking uncontrollably. Our receptionist, who had a huge heart, told me she had my back and told me she would take care of things, not to worry, not to come in, and she'd see me in the new year. I hung up the phone, barely saying a word. When I tried to speak, it came out as half words or mumbled blurbs. I was standing outside myself, and words couldn't form.

Everything became a fuzz after this. From this moment, the world as I knew it was altered. I was shattered. It was all gone from everything I believed to everything I thought that mattered. The one person who I would have reached out to for these exact matters was now gone, nowhere to be seen, and I was shocked and didn't know where to go next, what to do or who to turn to.

This intensity of grief had struck me harder. I had lost people before, my grandparents and Steve, but this was different. It was like a domino effect of everyone I had ever lost before. On top of that, losing Mary was like losing a limb. She was a part of me, like my other half. Who was I going to be without her? I was afraid to find out.

****

The swirling winds of grief took me out. I couldn't eat, I couldn't sleep, and I lived off homoeopathic Bach Rescue Remedy. Staring at the wall became a norm for me. Hours would pass by, and I didn't even budge. I hated sleeping, and nothing was funny. I wouldn't say I liked the feeling of waking up in the morning and having a moment of stillness before reality struck me again. Mary was still gone, she was still dead, and I was still here, without her.

Without knowing who I was or who to turn to for a talk. I found comfort in sitting with her mother. We cried and held each other's arms. Very few words were spoken, as there was nothing to say. Mary died of a tragedy, something that could have been preventable if it had been treated early on. But the emergency department turned her away, with her mother being accused of being an overcautious parent. Apparently, it was only the flu. But her mother knew. She even asked the emergency doctor if this could have been meningitis, as it just came on so strong. From the moment she was sent home to the moment she passed away, it was probably 12 hours. Mary was still gone, we were still here, and no amount of reliving the story or blaming the hospital for their mistake would make her come back. I had to come to terms with it, and I had to find my way without her. When my other close friend Crista died three months later from another unknown medical condition, it was too much. Unfortunately, I was in such a fog that it only added another burden on top of me that I didn't know I could handle. Somehow, though, I did manage to speak at her Celebration of Life.

My only wish was that I could be in the future, a couple of years from that moment, so the pain I was feeling would wear off, and I wouldn't be hurting so much.

I started searching. I talked to anyone and everyone about finding some comfort or spiritual connection to something. I didn't grow up in a religious home. I was steered away from religion as my dad didn't want us involved in Catholicism as he had very strong opinions about it. He wanted us to find our own spiritual path. I had been curious my whole life about who God was and where I went when I died. Losing Mary and Crista just made me even more curious.

I talked to Jehovah's Witnesses, joined a Christian Bible study, and participated in Buddhist meditations. I aimlessly walked into churches, attended services, tried to take communion, and drank the chalice of wine with the priest. But studying the Bible wasn't for me, I felt it was too dogmatic. There was too much focus on what the book said instead of having a direct experience with God. I didn't want a book that promised me an afterlife in heaven, I wanted the real thing now and to understand where they went. So, I went to Russell Books in downtown Victoria, BC, and read books about crossing over. James Van Praagh, the medium, had a few books about death, dying and mediumship. I read what I could, a lot of it washed over me. All I knew was that I was willing to try it all. I was at rock bottom, and my parents didn't know how to help me. Grief therapy did help as my therapist taught me how to journey and meet my friends in another realm within a guided meditation. I kept going and doing the best I could.

About four months after Mary passed, I had a dream. Mary came to me. She climbed into my bed and started shaking me, trying to wake me up.

"PSSST", she whispered loudly.

"What?" I answered as I rolled over in my sleep.

She stood before me. She was rocking me, trying to wake me up. In my sleep state, I looked right at her, put my hand up and said, *"I can't, you're dead",* and rolled back over, annoyed and frustrated.

"PSSSSST!" she said even louder. Trying to get my attention, she pushed me harder. *"IT'S ME!"*

"Noooooo!" I said back to Mary as I threw the covers over my head in my sleep state. *"You're dead! Go away!"* I was

annoyed I was having a dream. Sleep was the worst part of the day for me, for when I woke up, I had to accept that my friends were no longer with me and not coming back.

"Hey, it's Mary. Want to come with me on an adventure?"

"Mary, you're dead! Leave me alone; it's hard enough, I'm just dreaming," I said, mumbling under my breath, hoping this would end soon.

"It really is me. I guess I'll have to prove it to you." She took the blanket beneath me and reefed it. In that action, I flipped off the bed and landed on the floor, smacking the ground. My eyes shot open in disbelief at what happened.

My mom came running into the room and swung open my door, finding me on the floor with blankets on top of me in the middle of the night. *"What happened?"* she asked in surprise as she stood at the door.

"It was Mary; she was here. She just pushed me off the bed! She wanted to prove it was really her." I answered, surprised at what was coming out of my mouth.

"Believe it." my mom said as she raised her eyebrows, gave me a look and then closed the door and went back to her room.

I climbed back into my bed, shocked. Could that really have been Mary? Was she actually visiting me in my sleep? The thoughts swirled around my brain as I drifted back to sleep.

Many nights after that, Mary visited me as I dozed off to sleep. She would take me away as if I was Wendy following Peter Pan to Neverland. I knew it was her, from her proof of pushing me off the bed and my mom validating it with the look she gave me. I embraced her in my dreams and it felt more real than ever. Mary would take my hand as I drifted off, and she would take my spirit body to the other side to the spirit world. We did this many times, so much so that we even had a meeting place.

"Did you think I'd just leave you hanging like that?" she asked me.

"Well, yeah. You were gone."

"Maybe from Earth, but I am more alive than ever over here", she smiled.

"Why did you leave?"

"You knew I wouldn't live a long life," she said to me with a wink.

She was right, Mary often talked about leaving life early. She told me she wouldn't have much of an adult life and would die young like her aunty. She said it wasn't her purpose to grow old but to be young. I always thought that was a crazy thing to say. But she would always tell me where we would meet up in Heaven. She told me on walks when we were 14 that we would ride bikes one day in spirit. We would lay with the lions and drink honey milk from the rivers flowing through the valley. It all sounded like a fantasy, but I always went along with it. Why not? It made death exciting and made me feel like it was something to look forward to.

Mary wasn't afraid of death. She would tell me that she actually couldn't wait to be home again. Visiting her in my dream state while she was in spirit gave me a preview of what it would be like on the other side.

In the dreams we saw so many sunrises and sunsets on a bank, watching the ocean crash waves into the shore. We would walk through shopping malls, looking at all the clothes coming into fashion shortly. We both loved shopping, and that was something we always did together.

She told me she promised me that she would let me know she was okay after she died. Dreaming was the easiest way to reach me, and she told me she came to comfort me that she wasn't gone. She also needed me to see where she was and that she was more alive than ever.

These dreams lasted for several weeks, periodically, until I felt better. I started to develop a clearer understanding of where she was, and although I was here, nothing could separate us. She was just in another realm, living out her next evolution of soul growth. She was with the angels, she used to tell me. Not ever for a moment did I feel that she was with anything but them.

When the dreams stopped, I felt an incredible amount of power and strength running through me. Something was giving me this strong sense to live, and I knew I needed to be living my life fully. The grief was no longer consuming me, but a deep willingness for life started to settle in. I knew Mary was with me, and I was meant to be here. I was never the same and began to like that depth about me. Nine months after she died, I left my job as a hairstylist and bought a plane ticket to travel the world solo. I was gone for 12 months and travelled to Australia, New Zealand, Thailand, Cambodia and Fiji. It was time to start appreciating the life I had been given to live. So I did and lived it up.

Dream Or Visitation

Dreams are a relevant way for spirit communication. You are out of the way when you are asleep, so it creates room to answer prayers and let spirit in. This is a common way for you to receive guidance about where we are headed and a way for your loved ones in spirit to communicate with you to let you know they are okay.

When I speak to clients, they often tell me they would do anything for a dream of a loved one. Usually, they receive one when they least expect it and it's incredibly healing. They are just there in the dreams, but the unexpected makes it so special.

So, what is the difference between a visitation from a loved one or just a dream?

When we dream, we work out what we haven't unravelled in our waking state. That's why our dreams can be metaphorical and symbolic. They don't always make sense to the human mind, but our minds let go when we sleep. That is why we usually feel better when we wake up. You will notice with dreams that you can't always remember them. You may remember it vividly when you wake up, but by midday, it's already starting to fade. The more you try to remember it, the less and less you can grasp what happened.

You are still sleeping when you have a visitation, but you remember everything. It feels so real that you even wonder how this is possible in your sleeping state. You see them, feel them, and remember specific details, messages and locations. Even the thought of the visitation gives you goosebumps on your arms as it feels like they are actually there. When you have visitations, they are real. It means your loved one in spirit (or guides) came to visit you, leave you a message, say hi, comfort you, let you know they are okay where they are, or help you here. Usually, this event will be a shifting force in your healing journey, igniting or changing something for you from here forward.

Usually, visitations don't happen often. Maybe a one-off or a handful of times. They are meeting points in the dream state to help you in your waking state. I have met people who have never had them, while others who have had a few. Again, this has to do with your ability to let go when you sleep and the way your loved ones in spirit or guides choose to reach you. Sometimes, your loved ones in spirit find other ways to communicate, so visitation dreams aren't necessary.

When Mary died, and I started having visitations from her, I knew I was incredibly blessed to have these experiences. She familiarised me and maybe even planted seeds for my future direction. At that point, I had no idea what a medium was or how to commune with the afterlife. Visiting Mary in those meeting spaces was incredibly powerful and awakening for me, so much so that I went from a deep depression, in a state of grief, feeling hopeless in despair about the world, to feeling motivated and inspired with inner strength. To this day, those visitations feel like a part of my life, and the vivid memories are like real-life ones. They are so strongly embedded in my memory as a pivot point for my life.

I recommend asking Spirit always to find ways to help you with your grief. Ask for dream visitations if you can't feel their presence around you, as it will be a way for you to get out of the way enough to receive them. Ask Spirit to guide you in your waking life to show you ways to connect with them.

An intentional prayer to use:

"Great Spirit, please help me in my grief. Show me my loved ones in spirit are with me even when I can't see them myself. Open my blinders and take away any barriers to what Spirit is trying to show me. Let my loved one in spirit come in a visitation so I can remember. Help me transform my life with grace and ease. Thank you, amen."

Something Spirit has shared with me is why visitations don't happen often or why they happen when you least expect it. I have received the answer that it's important to live your life here on Earth. If you have too many visitations, your sense of missing them may heighten, making it unbearable to be here. You may also lose touch with your life and become more connected to the spirit world. You need to live your life fully here, but receiving messages, guidance and love from them gives you that boost to continue moving forward.

How Come I Can't Feel You Around Me?

Often, when I talk to people who are suffering in their grief, they share with me that they don't feel their loved ones in spirit around them and they don't understand why. Every morning, when they wake up, they ask for a sign that day. They ask to feel their loved ones in spirit around them and they don't. This usually adds to their suffering, feelings of loss and can make people feel alone.

When a client comes to see me for a reading, I can usually feel a barrier when a loved one in spirit comes through whom they deeply long to connect with and are unbearably missing. It's as if their grief is so heavy that it creates an energetic wall that blocks them. Of course, this is unconscious and they don't even know they are doing this. As a medium, it's an interesting observation, especially as the person wants to know why they can't feel their loved one around them.

When connecting with a spirit, the medium connects to them on a high vibration of love. Through that frequency, they can bring forth information and evidence of who they are connecting with, so they are recognisable, along with a message of what they are trying to say to their loved one still here.

The vibration of love is a very high frequency. Picture a fan on at full speed spinning. It goes so fast that you cannot see the individual blades, but you can see them fully when stopped. Grief is a low vibration. Even though it is completely necessary to feel and a part of the process as you have to go through it, grief can also make it difficult to connect with someone who has crossed over if this is your dominant emotion.

With this awareness, there can be a tendency to want to escape grief, as though it is a mistake. Some people end up hating feeling grief so much that they use substances to take the pain away (alcohol, marijuana, shopping, gambling, etc.) Unfortunately, it only temporarily dulls the pain before it returns. Grief is a sign you have loved. What we are inviting in is the gradual acceptance of grief, which comes with allowing yourself to feel it and turn it into something beautiful through some form of self-expression. Those who have come to a deep acceptance of grief can still experience it coming and going but are no longer prisoners to it and can still connect with their loved ones. It is in the moments of surrender that they can draw close. Every human emotion needs to be felt in life for it not to have power over you and control your life (hence how substance use gets involved). All feelings are good and have a place.

The fact that grief is a low vibration does not make it wrong, and knowing that you can't fake yourself out of it is essential. You cannot pretend to be all happy and smiley, as your energy vibration does not lie. As you feel your emotions fully, your vibration naturally does rise. This is why it's so important to feel your grief fully, as you cannot skip this process if you want to feel better and move forward with your life.

How do I keep my heart open when I am grieving?

Raising your vibration is a practice of becoming mindful of your feelings and recognising that each feeling and thought has a vibration. When you lose a loved one, it can be incredibly painful, both physically and mentally. It can also be a key to a huge awakening in your life as you go through it entirely, taking it as an opportunity to learn and grow spiritually.

It is important to feel your emotions and seek supportive environments to help you. Finding like-minded people who have been through something similar and who understand and have seen their way through the situation will help, as will having stability around you so that you don't overwhelm yourself. Eating healthy/properly, sleeping regularly, and remembering to exercise and get outside to try and walk daily (weather pending, of course, speaking as a Canadian!) will all help you move the heavy energy.

When you are grieving, you will need to find things to lift your spirits, as sometimes you will not be strong enough on your own to find that within yourself. Changing your environment for an hour can quite quickly shift your mood. Play uplifting music, dancing, watching comedy, playing with animals, filling your home with plants, or going for a walk in nature. Be mindful of your thoughts, asking the Creator to help show you another way, a different perspective you haven't thought of before. To open your mind and work with you directly. Talk to spirit often, ask for help to uplift you, and pray for mercy and grace when it feels unbearable. You have to remember your emotions are just energy moving through you, and energy flows; it's not permanent or stuck. As a part of nature, we are always changing and adjusting. To get into the flow, you need to move with the current of life.

When you get stuck on thoughts or beliefs, talk them through, be expressive and do something creative, and make sure you are being kind to yourself. Choose to learn from your situation and grow consciously. Grief is a hugely transformational experience in life, and when you are isolated in that state, it can be deadly. Let your grief keep your heart open. Something so devastating can rock your world, but something will always be there to deepen your connection to your higher power. That is what grief is all about. Your love for your loved ones can be so intense that the only thing that can compare to that love is letting the Divine fill your heart. Nothing will fill that void in the same way. Opening your heart will fill you with strong divine love and help you find a connection to your loved ones in spirit that you have craved. Finding joy in grief can become the most precious gift you discover in your life.

I also found huge comfort in spiritual circles, and this is how I discovered Spiritualist Churches/Centres. Through my early 20s, when I was dealing with grief, I always reached for spirituality, for I had to find a deeper understanding of life. The Spiritualist Churches/Centres were a way for me to seek understanding, comfort and like-minded people. Let's be honest, you will definitely meet someone in Spiritualism who understands grief, as that usually brings people through the door.

Raising your vibration helps you see things from a higher perspective, as you can have the same experience with a completely different perspective. Set your intention to raise your vibration and be conscious about moving your energy up instead of staying down.

For example, being home alone at night can be freedom in one state of mind or loneliness in another. Being mindful of your thoughts, and seek to understand your emotions and how you feel, for it allows you to be more present with life and to feel alive. When you feel bad, avoid watching shows with violence or visual trauma that make you feel worse. It will only feed on your experience and add to your negative spiral.

You Need To Believe It To See It

"It is better to believe than to disbelieve; you bring everything to the realm of possibility." - Albert Einstein

It's easy to search too hard, looking for solid proof that there is an existence beyond this plane. An attitude of *'I'll believe it once I see it'* and *'I need concrete proof to know it exists'* means that until your mind is satisfied that it has the evidence it needs, it won't believe in the afterlife. And even with overwhelming evidence, that same mind can still dismiss it. Yet, when communing with spirit, you are working with the non-physical, which cannot be measured.

When you shift your perception to believe first, you will notice that proof is all around you. You only have to think for a moment about the fact that we live on a planet amongst the stars. You got here without human effort, as the Earth existed before and without us. It's easy to get focused looking for something to look a certain way, limiting your reach. Things don't happen when you demand or make them, they happen when you intend lightly, then let go and allow room for it to fall in, usually when you least expect it to.

For example: When waiting to hear back about a job interview, does it happen when you are waiting by the phone and obsessing about it, checking your phone every 5 seconds? Or does it happen when you actually take your mind off it and do something productive? It's your lightness that allows room for things to open. When you are tight, in resistance and controlling, you don't create space for your intentions to come in. It's like gripping water- it falls through your fingers. When you cup water lightly, it can fill your whole hand. When you are demanding to life, you meet resistance. When you tell the world how it will be in force, the world humbles you and quickly. When you are open and receptive, the most incredible miracles can occur. Ever wonder why amazing things happen to other people but maybe not you? Practice letting go of your demands or tending to your intentions lightly. Then let go and let spirit take it from there.

I have had readings where clients have come and dismissed everything brought through in the reunion with their loved ones in spirit. They were waiting for "real proof" with the pre-arranged secret code they had with their loved ones in spirit before they died. For example, the loved one says, *'I will have the medium say the word alligator.'* The medium then fails to say that magical word but provides ample evidence they have the loved one in spirit. But, because the client has not heard this magic code word, they can dismiss everything else said.

I try not to eye roll these days, knowing TV has taught people that this is something to do to test a medium. Spirit will bring you the evidence and the message you need, based on the medium's ability and the recipient's readiness. A strong desire or want can block the miracle of the evidence and message that is presented to you in impeccable timing if you hold too rigidly to it. If you do not believe in the existence of the Divine, you may not be open enough to receive what is right in front of you, as the cynical mind will discredit it.

I have this joke with mediumship that if I am too accurate in bringing through a loved one in spirit, I may be called a fraud. And if I am not bringing exactly through what they want and in the order they want it, I may be too vague or a general medium. So, I cannot wait for the opinion of others to tell me how to do this work. It is up to spirit, my willingness to empty and become a vessel, and stay open to what is being guided through, as it's none of my business anyway. Spirit is in the driver's seat, my job is to stay out of the way. When my mind gets in and tries to look clever, it spoils the whole communication.

Often, when those pre-planned secret codes and messages pop in within a reading, it is because the person is open to the experience and not hung up on it. It's an added bonus to the reading, but it wasn't expected to happen. You must come with an open mind, knowing that spirit knows far better what you need to hear, instead of high expectations of how it should be with the arms crossed, saying, *"When I see it, then I'll believe it."* That's backwards!

When communing with spirit, let yourself become guided as you offer your intentions and follow the pull of your heart. Allow room for your prayers and requests to be heard and reciprocated—the how and why are unimportant.

You need to feel and imagine what you'd like but let go of how it will happen. The more you try to figure things out, the more stress and resistance you create to getting there.

There is an intelligence that lies in this universe, your job is to get into alignment with it. Let go of how it needs to play out and manifest. Spend more time looking in awe of the creation around you and all that is. In that appreciation, more will come to you. As what you appreciate expands and spirit can come closer in openness.

Gift Or Ability

Every human being has the ability to learn to listen to their intuition. When you think of life before technology, when people were deeply connected to the Earth and didn't have the science to back things up, they relied heavily on their intuition. Being connected to yourself is not a gift; it's a life skill. Learning to live from the heart and being led is something you are born with, but just living life can lead to feeling numb and questioning yourself. Traumatic situations, wanting to fit in, and listening to authorities are all ways you lose touch with your intuition and start questioning everything, putting too much in your head.

Intuition is trainable and teachable, and over time, people can re-introduce their intuitive selves and live more in harmony with their intrinsic nature. Growing your intuition is listening to your body and seeing how it responds.

Does this feel good?

Do I feel called to do that?

Why am I going through with this even though it doesn't make sense logically, but I feel strongly about it?

These are ways we learn to trust our intuition and be guided from within.

Intuitive abilities, where you know things about other people, will naturally begin to develop as you become more in tune with yourself. This is empathising, where you are aware of your surroundings and listen from within on how to read the situation. It's also possible to develop the ability to receive messages and to have premonitions of people. This usually stops people from developing their abilities further, as they don't want to know certain things or they don't want to be given that type of information. I completely understand this, and it's our free will, as I don't want to know things about the people I love in my life if it will cause them harm. But it is part of your development skills to learn to use your power of intention to choose which information you want to let in or not. You hold the power to make that decision.

You have to learn to ask to use this ability for the highest good, as opposed to being open to receiving just any information. It's about being open to information that aligns with you and is helpful, healing and guided. Think of a radio station... do you want to listen to inspiring, uplifting channels? Or do you want to listen to the radio station sharing everything wrong with the world, falling apart and making you feel worse about yourself and humanity. Remember, you get to make that choice. Just like you can grab the remote on a TV and shut the news off or change the channel, you can also turn off or change stations in your intuitive senses.

Now, mediumship, communicating with loved ones in spirit who have passed on, is different. As I said, intuition is an ability, a life skill to learn, but you cannot always choose to see spirits. There are a few ways this can happen. One situation is when a medium is born, meaning they bring this ability with them into this lifetime. Even as a young child, they were aware of spirit around people and were born highly sensitive (maybe hereditary or from another lifetime).

The second is when a trauma cracks you open. This means you are living your life, then all of a sudden, something significant happens to you, such as the death of a loved one, a health crisis, a dramatic breakup, or a natural disaster and your mediumship ability cracks open. Often, I find when this one happens that there was already a high sensitivity within or a born ability, but the person had it closed off, and in the trauma it re-awakened.

The third situation is a heavy interest and curiosity in mediumship. I have had students come to class wanting to develop their intuition. Over time, with consistency, dedication, and immersion with other students, their evidential mediumship ability unfolds naturally. This one is less common, as I find it's the dedicated ones that consistently come to circle for a couple of years that this happens to, and not everyone has that patience.

All three ways open up on their own accord. You cannot force mediumship to open. You cannot decide overnight that that's what you want to do. It has to come from within to develop, and you have to be patient with it as it unfolds. Seeing spirit is one thing, but learning how to communicate the needs and evidence of spirit is another.

Is mediumship an ability to be learned, or is it a gift? I find this a paradoxical question. On the one hand, you are developing an ability, stretching a muscle, and growing your sensitivity. However, if you treat it like nothing, like anyone can learn this, you may take it for granted or not see the actual miracle that is taking place. If you connect to mediumship as a gift, you will treat it like a gift. Those who I see do this have more of a special, intimate relationship with it. As with any gift, you take care of it, are grateful for it, and nurture it.

I was born a highly sensitive child. I was telepathic with animals and nature. I have communed with spirit in my backyard since I was 5 + years old. I was born into a life where communicating with spirit was natural and it felt like it was a part of who I was. However, it wasn't until Mary died and then I had my close call with death in the emergency room that my life path moved in the direction of greater energy awareness. When I applied myself to 3 years of training at Langara College in Integrative Energy Healing and started understanding myself and developing a relationship with energy, I consciously started to open up with skill and discipline.

In 2013, I visited England with my now husband Matthew, and we were hanging out with my brother-in-law. He takes the most amazing photos. He has an eye for it, he knows. I remember telling him that he had a gift for photography and that, despite technological advances, not everyone could take the kind of pictures he could. I remembered my own words when I started developing my mediumship. If I had treated it like anyone could do this, I would deny or dismiss the miracle that was happening. But if I saw it as a gift, I would cherish it more. So, I did.

Chapter 2: Empowerment

~

Give Your Power To No One

"When someone shows you who they are, believe them the first time." - Maya Angelou

2011-2012

When I started my path looking for spiritual teachers, I was young and too inexperienced to know what I should be looking for in a mentor. I knew that my hairdresser career was ending, as I no longer had the passion I used to, but I also had this strong calling from within; I was on a path of transformation and spiritual healing.

When I started my 3-year training at Langara College studying Integrative Energy Healing, I was introduced to many amazing teachers who held integrity, grounding and teachings that opened me up and put me on this path. Even though I was growing on a solid path, I was still like a kid in a candy shop, totally curious about what else was out there. I was enthralled by spirituality. I wanted to know everything and anything I could get my hands on. In my exploration, I came across Shamanism. I wanted to learn how to grow a deeper relationship and connection to the Earth and use my gift of sensitivity with Spirit communication.

I heard about a Celtic Shaman from England who had recently relocated to British Columbia and ran these underground circles out of his home. My lineage is from the UK and parts of Europe, so this path felt like it would be good and culturally appropriate. I wanted to understand my ancestry better and become more connected to the Earth. Frankly, I was curious about where my healing abilities and connection to Spirit were coming from. So, I started showing up at the weekend workshops he held in Vancouver.

At this point in my life, I was living in Squamish. I attended many ritualistic ceremonies that fascinated me, primarily because of how mysterious the shamanic leader Jean Pierre was. He was a bit of an oddball, but as a shaman, I'm pretty sure he'd take that as a compliment. His ceremonies were theatrical and enriching, and he would spend hours putting them into production. He fully embraced the personality of his astrological sign of Leo. I approached him about taking his 3-year mentorship and training under him. Although he welcomed me in, he was always quite distant with me, too.

Every month, I would drive to his house for a sacred circle and spend the weekend at house, which looked like a fairy forest, with 5 or 6 other people. Here, we would practice rituals and journeying, learning techniques for soul retrieval, healings and guidance into the underworld. To this day, I still take a lot that I learned from him. It wasn't so much what he taught or the education of what he was teaching, but the immersion of being there with like-minded individuals.

One thing that bothered me was that, after training at Langara College, I had gotten used to teachers of such high quality and integrity that I questioned them when I believed that teachers didn't match that level. I noticed Jean Pierre liked to gossip about the other students and talk about their personal lives as if we were his entertainment. So, I stayed really quiet with him. I never wanted to be the source of his gossip in his other groups, so I didn't feel safe sharing a lot.

He wanted us to get tattoos on our arms to show commitment to our path. I passed and was conveniently sick that weekend…

He felt my distance and would make comments to me like, *"Oh, Nicole, you are just a light worker."* What was supposed to be an insult I took as a compliment. When I looked around, I noticed that many of his other students didn't look entirely healthy and maybe a little addicted to the dark. Even though I wasn't perfect nor one to judge, I noticed the longer people stayed under his leadership, the more their personal issues, health issues and possible addiction issues would escalate. Even though I had made friends with some people there and looked up to them, I felt something was incredibly off about a lot of it and how it was run.

Jean Pierre would comment, saying that we were still in the fun phase of his mentorship- making drums and practising ceremony. But it wouldn't be long before our lives would turn upside down, and we'd take up smoking before we realised how much we'd need his guidance. I thought that was odd. Why would we want us to get sicker? Weren't we supposed to be getting better? I started having nightmares and noticing that in each of my terrors, he was always in my dream. I would email him, asking him what the heck was going on. Why was he in my sleep last night, shoving snakes down my throat and telling me to swallow? I would get these short emails telling me that this was part of my unfoldment and that I needed to walk bravely into the dark, not to be afraid of it. Most of the work we did was in the dream world anyway. My eyebrow would raise, wondering if I could go dark enough to find the light. It sounded a bit backwards if you asked me.

After a few weeks of these night terrors, we were in class, and I asked him if Shamanism was a path to enlightenment. He laughed, then paused. He then shared that Shamanism wasn't about enlightenment at all but about being of service.

I didn't understand. Nor did I really want to. I felt confused and untrusting of him, yet I didn't want to say much because I didn't like being the source of his gossip. Nor did I want to feel like I wasn't strong enough to walk this path. He preached that he created warriors that weren't afraid to walk in the dark, and yet, I saw some crippled, sick students who had a heavy reliance on him.

At the end of our first year of mentorship, our small group was invited to a 5-day Shamanic Conference he was part of. We were invited to partake in and watch the initiation ceremony he was doing for his graduates in his mentorship program. I was curious what the graduates would be like, and I was also interested in what vows the students would say in their initiation into this Shamanic Path.

We gathered in this octagon-shaped indoor-outdoor space. A fire pit in the middle had a hole in the ceiling so the smoke could go up and out. He had his students graduating from his apprenticeship dressed in black robes at the front. He lit torches and the fire pit and poured gas on the concrete in a circle all around his graduating students and him; they were within the circle. He took his BBQ lighter, lit the gas, and lit the circle in flames. There they were, within this circle of a burning fire around them.

He pulled out a binder with the vows he would have his students repeat after him. But before he did that, he gave each of them a drop on their tongue from a glass bottle with a dropper. It was to put them in an altered state of consciousness, like a mood-altering substance- plant medicine. I am unsure which one it was or if it was his concoction. The drummers drummed, the students wigged out, and after about 15 minutes, when everything kicked in and everyone was trancey, he started having the students repeat after him the vows they were making to their commitments in shamanism and, most importantly… to him.

I sat there by myself with my arms crossed. I felt like an outsider amongst the outsiders. I was aware everyone who walked in the path of shamanism was an outsider, but I felt like an outsider to the max because I didn't want to get too close to the vibes. I didn't trust him.

There were shamans from all around the world at this shamanic conference. Europe, the UK, the USA, Africa, Australia- you name it. It was a 5-day conference, and those who walked this path around the world could come to gather and share knowledge.

I listened as he had the students repeat after him. All seemed normal until he had them say, *"And if you ever leave Jean Pierre on this path of Shamanism, you will be cursed 10,000 lifetimes."*

I listened as his students repeated after him without fail… *"Oh… My… God…"* I said to myself under my breath. *"I am in a fucking cult!"* That was my perception of it anyway. There is, of course, a lot more to cult dynamics, but this was how I made sense of it at the time.

My eyes bugged out of my head. I scanned the room and saw that everyone was entranced, watching the show being indoctrinated and performed in front of them. This was sick, and no one was protesting it. Of course, maybe they were sitting there like me, thinking this was insane, and where's the escape route? But they were all surrounded by the fire ring around them, the black robes, the substance that put them in an altered state and then this classic Jean Pierre performance telling them to repeat the vows. This was real. He knew what he was doing (he had a Ph.D. in psychology), and I wanted no part of it.

At that moment, I prayed, *"Spirit, if you want me here, lean me forward. If you want me gone, pull my energy back."* Within seconds, while in the ceremony, the two back legs of my plastic outdoor furniture chair split in half, and I flew backwards onto the ground. There I was, feet in the air, head on the ground behind me, looking straight up at the ceiling. I started giggling and almost cackling intently because I got my immediate answer. Most of the people were so entranced in the ceremony that only a few noticed and helped me up.

"Holy smokes!" I thought, *"I couldn't have gotten a clearer answer."*

As I got up, I started making my way to the back of the room, leaving the broken chair in the middle of the crowd untouched. It felt more like a statement. When I got to the back of the room, I was met with a woman I vaguely recognised who was in the Integrative Energy Healing Program I took at Langara and graduated a few years ahead of me. She looked at me as if knowing what I had asked to Spirit and seemed to know what I was thinking. I looked at her, and she said under her breath, *"RUN"*.
I walked out of the building, apparently during the big show. Of course, like any sacred ceremonial event, it's customary to hold space and not leave the room when in a ceremony.

But I had no trust, didn't care and left anyway. The event ended quickly after I walked out. I noticed a few of the women who were elders in the tradition following me. They wondered what I was doing. I said to them that not in a million years would I ever say those vows to Jean Pierre, so my work here was done.

"What vows?" One of the elders spoke. She looked at me as if I didn't understand what the big deal was.

"Uh, you will be cursed 10,000 lifetimes if I ever leave Jean Pierre?" I said back. *"Those words will never come out of my mouth."*

She laughed and waved her arm at me. *"Oh Nicole, it's just words! He doesn't actually mean that; it's more for the show. You know, to make it dramatic. No one actually believes that."*

"No way", I retorted, as I shook my head. No part of me ever felt to conform that way, even if it meant walking out of a tribe, a new spiritual family and way of life I was included in.

She then told me that if I really didn't want to say that, I could cross my fingers behind my back, as that reverses word vows.

I shook my head again, knowing without a doubt that there was no way in hell I would ever be able to step foot in the circle again. I walked off the property, knowing I had dodged not only a bullet but a curse, and I walked home. I gathered all the belongings I had accumulated with Jean Pierre over the year and broke them in half as I built a bonfire and burned them. I needed to cut all ties, all spells, all curses or whatever juju was connected to him. It was a knowing. I did keep my drum because it felt like mine, but every other lock and key had to go fast.

I followed up with an email to Jean Pierre that I needed to talk to him about continuing after the conference.

He wrote back to me immediately, wanting to chat now. I let him know that I was moving to Victoria on Vancouver Island (which I was) and that I didn't want to continue. Oh, and PS: I would never say those vows I witnessed in that ceremony to you.

It was done. He wrote back a quick goodbye, and it was over.

I never spoke to or had contact with him again, and I noticed that many of his followers and students left in the bunches, too, in the coming months after that event. I left at the right moment and felt okay staying as long as I did. I believe my intuition guided me the whole time, as I needed that experience to know in my heart what is right from wrong when it came to Spiritual Teachers. At some point in his life, I believe he was a good man, maybe, but he just went really dark. I can forgive him for that. But I was unafraid to speak up for myself and what wasn't a fit. It has helped me detect these things moving forward in my life and for my clients, students and even congregation members.

As a minister, I know I hold a lot of power, and I do my best to make sure people know they are responsible for themselves and do not give me their power. We each have to hold our own, and my job is to give you back your power so you can reclaim it and rediscover it within yourself.

Spirit Is Love

"When I believe my thoughts, I suffer. When I question them, I don't. And, I've come to see this is true for every human being."- Byron Katie

When I worked with Jean Pierre in Shamanism, there was always something to cleanse, fix, heal, extract, remove, curse-unbind and protect myself from. We were right into the dark arts, and he encouraged us to dive straight in and trust no one. He would smile with glee, seeing us diving into the darkness. His mantra was, "*You must go into the darkness and face it head-on.*" I thought that the more into the darkness I'd go, the more there must be some light at the end of it. But the deeper I dug, the darker it got. I got sicker and noticed some other students weren't looking too hot either.

I'd often question Jean Pierre on his practices, wondering why things had to be so complicated, why we needed all this stuff (crystals, bells, shakers, feathers, rattles, costumes, skins, bones, decorated sticks and incense), and why we didn't just turn on the light. His response to me while sighing was that I was a bit too New Agey for him. To him, life wasn't about spreading light. It was about balancing energy with light and dark; I kept thinking he must have forgotten about the light part because, after a year, he still didn't mention anything about it. Over and over, he'd tell us, "*You mustn't be afraid of the dark*." I wanted to respond, "*You mustn't be afraid of the light*."

Now, as much as I felt deeply called and ancestrally pulled into shamanic work, and I understand what he was saying about balancing energies, it also felt like Jean Pierre was trying to get us dependent on him. He kept pushing us into our shadows, getting us to look at our flaws, our wounds, yet never providing any guidance on how to get out of it. We were being consumed by darkness instead of confronting it. He would often tell us that we hadn't gone into the darkness enough if we were still smiling and that only the strongest would be able to do this.

I was very resistant. Based on my formal training I had learned at Langara College what he was teaching had nothing to do with balancing the light and the dark. He was putting us at the bottom of the well of darkness, into our own self-obsession of looking at what's wrong with us rather than guiding us to find our gifts and strengths. I felt like I was caught up on a hamster wheel going around in circles rather than feeling like I was getting anywhere.

I often cringe today when I see people sucked into this kind of teachings that keep you floundering, stuck on the merry-go-round of constant healing and unworthiness and having something to look at and work on. Yes, of course, it is vital to develop a healthy relationship with yourself, your light and dark, but often, I see people get so infused with their shadow selves that they forget that they have some goodness in them, too.

Healthy shadow work is about recognising all aspects of self. It's about seeing the good, the bad and becoming observant of self. It's about making your darkness conscious. Allowing yourself to become a witness of your mind instead of believing all the thoughts you have about yourself. It's about seeing where you may project this onto the world, people in your life or even the spirit world. Ultimately, it's about learning to love all aspects of yourself unconditionally and bringing the power back to you to change.

As much as I agree with him that we cannot fear the dark as we need to be able to face ourselves and feel it all, it can quickly get out of hand, and our minds play a huge role in our own suffering. Jean Pierre told me that the shaman's path was one of the most gruesome initiations someone could go through, that only warriors could come through the other side, and that the spirits chose people.

I felt like I was always in battle, trying to peel the negative energy off of me or even entities I was taught that were around me and holding me back. It became real to me because that's what I practised, and that was what I was taught to do. But as I developed and shifted from these teachings that taught this way, my beliefs and understanding of the spirit world changed. Whatever you give your power to, whatever you believe and make real, you will build evidence for it. So, in that instance, yes, I made that my reality and it got really real, really fast.

That is so far from what I do, practice and/or teach today. You are responsible for what you choose to open up to and give your power to. When you start to develop an intimate relationship with the spirit world, you will begin to realise that there is pure love there, so much so that you will have to open yourself up to the amount of love that is trying to pour into you. I see this in teaching mediumship circle often with new students. They will be overwhelmed with the amount of love coming through from a loved one in spirit to who they are giving a reading to. Part of my guidance as a teacher is to help my students bring that love through in the reading as it's so easy to get overwhelmed. The spirit world isn't dark, that is a projection onto a realm that only has true love to give. People can be dark, but we live in a world of free will and choice. In my experience, I have seen spiritual people struggle with worthiness, shutting off the valve of pure love that is trying to pour into them from the divine.

The only thing real in this universe is love. Everything else is an illusion.

And as the famous words Wayne Dyer used to love to say, "*If you change the way you look at things, the things you look at change*". And he is right, your world changes.

So remember this before you fill your world with things that are no longer necessary or needed in your spiritual growth.

The further you go into your personal growth and development, the more you realise your whole world is within you and you are there to meet yourself. You are the medicine.

Practice redirecting your thoughts to love and soothe yourself if you feel fear about spirit. Here are a few intentional questions you can ask to re-centre yourself.

Help me connect on a vibration of love.

How can I best be of service to bring through messages with love and meaning?

Please show me how I can bring more light into my life.

Grounding

As within, so without, as above, so below, as the universe, so the soul." - Hermes Trismegistus

Mediumship is about becoming a bridge between worlds, having one foot in each world - the spirit world and the earth plane. You have to have one foot anchored here to give grounded information and stay compassionate to the person to whom you are giving messages.

Quite often I see people training in mediumship but they have lost their footing in this world. This will make people flighty, anxious, too open, over-sensitive and often, when they bring through messages, it will sound more like gobbledygook than mediumship. Ungrounded mediums is one way mediumship can get a bad rep.

Becoming grounded is essential in your development and also will help you develop a more practical and concrete (evidential) relationship with the spirit world. Grounding is not just about balance, but it's about being able to effectively translate the information you receive from the spirit world into meaningful and healing messages for the physical world. Do not be fooled. Those who spend their whole time travelling the astral planes are not more connected to spirit than you. They may have lost their footing. We are here to have a human experience, and only when you can funnel the information you are receiving from the spirit through to the physical world does it bring meaning and healing to humanity.

Learning to become a bridge between worlds is a discipline, and you need to know how to become fluent in spiritual connection, but the key is feeling and being present in the moment. You cannot leave your body to connect to spirit and bring through evidential mediumship. You need to connect to spirit while present in your body and senses.

Grounding Exercise:

Sit in a chair with your feet flat on the ground beneath you.

Take a few deep breaths, connect with your body, and feel your feet flat on the floor.

Let your breathing slow down, and start to feel a connection to the earth. Feel the heartbeat of Mother Earth beat through your feet.

Feel the energy from your feet drop into Mother Earth. Some people visualise tree trunks melting into the earth, tethering you to the centre of the Earth. Others feel the energy as you drop deep into the earth.

Feel connected. Feel one with the earth beneath you. Be in your body while you do this. Let it feel safe to do so.

You will know when you are grounded when your thoughts soften, you can feel the chair beneath you, your feet on the ground and the clothing on your skin or the hair on the back of your neck. Relax into it and tell yourself it's safe to be in your body.

Practice grounding often and regularly. After a while, you will feel it immediately when you are not grounded. As a sensitive person, feeling grounded and connected to the earth will be your new favourite thing. When you are in your body and connected to the earth, you won't pick up or sponge up other people's energies all the time. You will be rooted in your own power and just aware of someone else's energy without taking it on. You will feel more empowered and in control of your body and senses.

Salt & Smudge

As an energy-sensitive person, not only is grounding life-saving, but so is learning how to manage your energy. When you are an empath (someone who feels others' emotions), knowing how to give back what is not yours is important. In my first career as a hairstylist, I was constantly bringing home bad moods, anger, and frustration when there was no reason for carrying it. I became a chameleon for whatever my clients felt and matched them in their energy. It happened so naturally that I didn't even know I was doing it.

Once I started doing energy healing, grounding and meditation, I started learning about giving back energy that wasn't mine to carry. I also discovered salt baths and smudging as a way for me to discharge energy. I do not take these practices for granted and highly recommend learning how not to take on other people's stuff. Once you know what it feels like to be in your own energy, you can become more mindful when taking on energy that's not yours and discarding it. Salt baths also help with smoothing out your energy if you are over-revved, feeling energy sensitive or overwhelmed.

Salt Bath Cleanse:

1-2 cups Epsom salts
1 cup baking soda
1/3 cup dead sea salt or Himalayan salt.

Ten drops of tea tree oil OR a cap full of apple cider vinegar.

Place one crystal in your bath with intention.
Usually, I place a quartz to absorb the energy.

If you want to place your mixed salts in a jar, you can set it on your window sill under a full moon and charge it up before using.

This is the ultimate "get out of my energy" bath. Great for cleansing, it is also great for soothing your nervous system.

Smudging:

You can smudge your house or yourself with herbs from your garden or buy them from your local spiritual store (sage, lavender, rose petals, sweet grass, mugwort, etc.). In First Nations traditions, they use sage, as it is used to cleanse someone's energy, clean the air or a build-up of energy in a space. Using fresh herbs from your garden can also be highly effective when done with intention and prayer.

Directions:

Take a bunch of herbs and place them in an Abalone shell.

Light the herbs and let the smoke build up.

Take a large feather to sweep over the smoke and direct the smudge where you want it to go. (To cleanse a room or cleanse your aura).

Say a prayer or use intention as you do this. For example, *"May this smudge be used to cleanse the energy of this space"* OR *"May this smudge be used to cleanse my auric field."*

Share your gratitude for the smudge and put the smoke out when finished. I like to use a rock and push it against the shell to put out the smoke.

The significance of the shell, feather, herbs, and smoke represents a balancing of the elements.

Shell: Water
Feather: Air
Herbs: Earth
Smoke: Fire

A New Life

"Always remember that when dusk arrives, it already has dawn in its womb." - Amma

June 30th, 2012

    I was 26 when I ditched the perceived cult, packed up my house, broke up with my boyfriend, had his parents buy me out, quit my job and career as a hairdresser, and moved out of Squamish. I moved back home to Vancouver Island, Victoria, BC, on my graduation day at Langara College ~ Integrative Energy Healing Program so I could move back in with my parents and start over. I wanted to be a healer and was done living my life as I knew it. I had completely outgrown my old life. I no longer could fit the role I was playing. To outside observers, it looked like I had it all, but when I let it go, I felt freer than I had my whole life.

The day I left Squamish, the clouds were dark and there was a torrential rainstorm. My friend Angela and I were driving back from our program's graduation ceremony. We were halfway home on our 2-hour drive, and I told her, *"I just can't do this anymore. I want to leave right now. I can't wait until everything falls into place before I leave."*

She looked at me and answered with something truly profound: *"Do it. Just leave."*

It didn't even occur to me that it was possible.

"Let's drive to your house right now, pack up the rest of your stuff, put it in your car and just leave. Message people later to cancel appointments. People will get over it."

Just as we spoke, the storm got stronger. Thunder and lightning filled the air, and we drove faster to get to my house and get the job done.

She helped me as we rummaged through the house and grabbed the last of my belongings. We packed my cat Leo loosely in the car, and I placed Ebony, my miniature poodle, on the seat next to me. I filled the car with blankets to make sure they'd be comfortable. The rest of my lime green Beetle Volkswagen was packed to the brim with the remainder of my belongings. Tears flowed as I realised this part of my life was done. I locked the door behind me, thanking God that my ex-boyfriend wasn't in the house while I was cleaning my stuff out, so I didn't have to see him. I was shaking with anxiety, feeling like this was the bravest thing I had ever done. I waved Angela off, stepped on the gas pedal, and floored it down the highway out of Dodge.

I arrived at the Horseshoe Bay Ferry terminal 45 minutes later. As I drove out of Squamish, the thunder and lightning storm broke, the sky cleared, and the sun beamed on my face. I saw a rainbow in the distance as if the entire weather was joining me in my transition. When I arrived at the ferry terminal, it just so happened a ferry was boarding. There were no wait times on this auspicious long weekend, and without even checking the clock or a minute to put my car in the parking lot to wait, I drove directly onto the ferry. That happening so effortlessly is about a one-in-a-million shot; ask anyone who makes the trip often.

I sighed in relief, knowing I had been brave enough to shift my life radically, and when I arrived, I would launch my career as a healer. I was ready to do this work.

Chapter 3: Allowing

~

The Healing Power Of Mediumship

"As you start to walk on the way, the way appears."- Rumi

I opened my private practice on July 3rd, 2012. I worked out of my parent's house in their family room. On my first week, I already had two clients booked in, and I was convinced my practice would be a revolving door once it opened. I had put in well over 300 hours of practical experience doing healings. I had done the coursework, the case studies, the papers, and the practicums. I was, in my eyes, a full-fledged healer just waiting for people to show up so I could help them find themselves and their way. In some ways, I did, and in other ways, it just wasn't enough. After the first month, I started incorporating oracle and tarot cards into my readings, noticing when I took the time to pull a card for someone that they really appreciated and enjoyed having a little reading. Not long into that, I noticed that when clients called to book an appointment, they even asked if I could do the reading, as they felt good around the healing bit but could use a little clarity. So, I did.

In the meantime, I apprenticed with a woman named Nazli in Victoria, going deep into the depth of tarot to further my education in learning these cards, as I felt I wanted more to offer my new clients. Just reading angel oracle cards felt like it was not enough. In a way, I always felt like I was led from one thing to another.

My business grew slowly but consistently. Sometimes, it was busier than others, but I could usually keep 1-3 clients a week doing healings and add-on readings. It was not enough to live on, so I also got a job working in a Drug and Rehabilitation Centre up the island in Cobble Hill, BC. Matthew (my now husband) and I moved up the island and relocated our lives, and I made my healing room out of one of the bedrooms in the house we rented. I made it work, keeping my job during the day and doing healings/tarot readings on evenings and weekends.

****

My grandmother passed away on October 23rd, 2014—a very memorable time for me when I was going through a major transition in my life. I had been running my energy healing and tarot business for over two years but was ready to step deeper into it. I wanted to dedicate my whole life to this meaningful work, and I was uninterested in having another part-time job to stabilise me anymore. I was ready to take the plunge and needed a push for take-off. My grandmother died suddenly from a heart attack in the early morning hours of the day. Moments after she died and I was notified, I felt a strength that wasn't there before. I had noticed in my life that when people I had loved died, after the shock and numbness wore off, I was left with undeniable strength. She had become a part of me, and I felt she had been given a vision of my life. She could see what I was doing and where I was going and needed to encourage me to get there.

My work-job life started to fall apart quite quickly after that. I noticed my desire to be at my day job was less inspired, but my passion and love for my spiritual work were also well-received in the community. I got taken off the Sunday roster at my day job and given a different day of the week to replace it with. The first thing I thought I would do with that Sunday now off was find a local Spiritualist Church. I had been to one in Vancouver in my early 20s but could never consistently attend a service because of my work schedule. Now, I was able to.

I discovered a Spiritualist Church 20 minutes from where I lived and really enjoyed going to service, feeling connected, and loving being within that community. I noticed that when I watched the mediums work, there was a feeling in me that I could do what they were doing by talking to deceased spirits. When I looked around the room, I could see, sense, and hear the spirits standing behind people sitting down and their loved ones standing over them. I also met a woman there named Lana Ryan. When I saw her stand up to give spiritual healings at the end of the service, I heard a whisper in my right ear that said, *"This will be your new best friend"*. That whisper was very much correct.

After the first time I came home from the Spiritualist Church, I was inspired by what I witnessed. Being in that kind of environment where loved ones in spirit were invited into the space, as well as acknowledged and communicated with, really revealed to me that even though I was practicing healings and tarot readings, there seemed to be a mediumship ability going on for myself that I never really fully comprehended the power of. Of course, I had always noticed spirits around people within my mind's eye and saw people's deceased loved ones standing with them in healing, but I saw that as more normal and part of life. Only when I witnessed a Spiritualist Service did I get just how cool it was to see the spirits, communicate their language, and share what they had to say through evidential information, validated by the person in the audience. I could see this was taking this work to a whole new level, one that I was instantly inspired to learn.

When Matthew came home from work that night, I told him what I had witnessed at the Spiritualist Church over dinner. He seemed slightly interested, and I asked him if I could practice what I saw. He seemed open but a bit skeptical. Of course, he was interested in what I had seen but wondered how it would work if I knew him and if he had shared stories with me about his deceased grandparents.

I convinced him anyway. I told him that if I was legit and could do this. I would bring something through only he or his family would know about.

After dinner, we sat in the living room, and I sat on the couch chair across from him. I closed my eyes, opened up, and immediately, I was met with a grandfather. I told Matthew I had his grandfather with him, and he showed me a chalkboard and his teaching. Matthew confirmed that, yes, he was a university professor. I also shared with Matthew that he was telling me that he loved to teach and share like Matthew does. And that not only did he write a book about his life in the war, but he also wanted his books shared or re-read by the family. Matthew confirmed that, yes, that was true. Then his grandfather said, *"And there is a box of my books collecting dust in the basement!"* Matthew laughed, unsure about that, but confirmed his grandfather would probably want the family to re-read his book or at least acknowledge them.

I wasn't able to hold the mediumship connection for very long, as it was my first formal try, but I felt really strongly about his grandfather communicating with me. Matthew was thankful for me trying and said that all was correct, but he was still not sure how much I was taking from my memory and how much could not be anything I knew.

When his mother called from England the following day, she called Matthew to let him know that some copies of his grandfather's book were found and collecting dust in his uncle's basement. It was word for word to what came through in the reading the night before. When Matthew hung up the phone, he told me what his mom said. To Matthew, that was the confirmation. Something I didn't know, but his grandfather had been trying to get the message across to a few family members.

I felt pleased with myself that it worked. I felt confident in what was delivered, and it felt easier than anything else I had done. All I had to do was say who I had, who they wanted to talk to, and what they were trying to really communicate with evidence.

Spiritual healings felt so layered, and tarot required a lot of memorising of the cards and trust in intuition. But mediumship, this felt natural. All I had to do was close my eyes and open up, and then the spirit showed up and shared the rest. It came so easily that I developed an instant hunger to learn more and practice. Mediumship was born in me…. but how would I learn more about it?

****

I went to the Spiritualist Church again the following week, totally enthralled by what was happening. I studied everything the medium said and how they linked to the spirits. As I left one day, there was a flyer on the wall of a "Message Night" with a panel of local mediums saying they would be giving mediumship messages. I bought my ticket right there and decided I'd go. I was sure if I went to one of those message nights, I'd get a message from my grandmother.

"I'd like to come to the young lady in the middle with the navy blue and white striped sweater. Sweetheart, I got your grandmother here. She's telling me she had problems with her legs, died from a heart attack, was the matriarch of the family, and was a force to be reckoned with." The man stated while pointing his finger directly at me.

I smiled happily, knowing for sure that he had my grandmother.

"Darling, she says you need to be standing here doing this work." He smiled and pointed at the stage.

The medium, Reverend Malcolm Gloster, was the one who passed me the message. He looked stunned. My grandmother, in spirit, had literally pushed him out of his chair and delivered that message without a doubt.

When the words had caught up with him of what he just said, he took a step back as if he suddenly slightly doubted what flew out of his mouth so confidently.

I said thank you to him, with red eyes and a huge smile.
"I don't know what this means, darling, but I hope you can understand what she meant," Malcolm said as he backed up and sat down.

I smiled. I knew exactly what he meant, and, at that moment, I had a strong knowing.

"Hmmm", I thought*, "I'm going to become a medium, but not just any kind of a medium- a Spiritualist Minister medium. Just like the man who spoke to me."* All of a sudden, I was taken back seven years to the angel in the emergency room who visited me when I was sick and lying in the hospital bed. She told me I would be led to do this work. I had never quite identified what "this work" was until this moment, seven years after I received that first message. But as those words flew out of Malcolm's mouth that I was to "do this work", I knew exactly what my grandmother meant, and finally, I knew what the angel meant. Those words shifted the direction of my life in an instant. My life would never be the same again…

Going to this new church (Cowichan Valley Spiritualist Church of Healing & Light in Duncan, BC) excited me. It added an element to my life that just wasn't there before. I felt an opening in my heart. It was a way to recognise my loved ones through my grief, but also, it had a feeling it brought me, like a sense of peace, a sense of being home.

After those first few visits to the Spiritualist Church in Duncan, I noticed some changes around our house, like knocking. I'd be in the kitchen making lunch, and suddenly, I'd hear knocking at the door. I'd check the front door, and nobody would be there. At first, it was pretty casual, but it got more intense after a few days of this. I'd hear knocking on the top floor of the house; I'd run upstairs and look, but no one was there. I thought it was just me. I felt that this was a way of spirit playing tricks on me, and once acknowledged, it would go away. But on the 5th day, it started to bug Matthew.

"You can hear it too?" I said to him.

Apparently, yes, he did. So much so that he got up to check the front door when the knocking started in the middle of the night. He couldn't believe no one was there, the knocking was loud and clear.

After the second night of the knocking, waking us up and me too tired to get up and check the door, he returned to the bed and said, *"You are going to have to do something about this. The knocking is calling you."*

I agreed. Doing tarot readings and energy healing wasn't enough anymore. I needed to take this to the next step. I needed to start diving more into the world of evidential mediumship. The spirits were beginning to show up around the table of my energy healings. My tarot readings were no longer just tarot readings but entourages of loved ones in spirit standing with them. Things were happening, knocks were happening, and I even had to tell my tarot clients that the knocking they were hearing in the background wasn't the door. It was… the spirits.

I saw on the news board that a psychic fair was coming up. I quickly asked if my name could be put on the list for a reading. I was ready to have 20 minutes with a medium now, to see who else would come through from my loved ones in spirit.

At this point, my tarot and Energy Healing business started picking up, and I was working towards this full-time. By going to the church, a light was ignited within me. Spirit was beginning to show up in all my healings, filling the room with their ancestors around the energy healing table. When I was doing tarot, I couldn't help but notice spirit people walking around the room. It was distracting. Sometimes, I'd be working so hard to focus on the cards in front of me, but the presence of spirit was so loud I couldn't concentrate. It was as if someone was banging pots and pans over my head while I was trying to read tarot cards.

The mediumship reading at the church psychic fair couldn't come fast enough, and when I got there, I was placed with the medium Pam Malt. I sat down with Pam, and she greeted me with a huge smile and hug as she cosied into her chair. Pam had recently returned from the Arthur Findlay College in England and still had the AFC glow that I would come to know so well. She told me she would close her eyes to go deep while she connected with spirit to see who wanted to step forward.

She closed her eyes and took a deep breath. A second later, she opened her eyes and blurted out, *"I have to invite you to my mediumship development circle. I will be starting an introductory group in 2 weeks' time. You must come!"* with an intense stare into my eyes.

I didn't even blink. *"Yes,"* I said, looking directly back into her eyes. No further details were necessary. I didn't care where it was, how long, how much it cost- any of it. My whole body shook and said *sign me up*, just like that. So afterwards, I did.

It was Mary that came through that day. Pam brought her through with the most accurate detail. From the stripped socks she used to wear up to her knees to her colourful personality, flower dresses, love for life, dancing free spirit and her quick death in the hospital while being surrounded by spirit.

She wanted to talk to me about her passing.

At this point in the reading (literally, all this happened within ten minutes of meeting Pam.) I was sobbing and going through an entire box of tissues.

"She wants you to know the whole room was filled with angels. And she so easily let go and was absorbed by the light." Pam explained.

She also shared how Mary used to come to me in my dream state and we'd have visits. Hearing this from someone who didn't know her made it all real for me. I started to see how mediumship was much more than trying to know the future, but a source of love and connection that no other form of healing or therapy has ever brought me, and so instantaneously.

A weight was lifted off my chest. Losing a young person in such a horrific way and under such sad circumstances was so hard. Those words brought peace to my heart. Years of stress melted away in a moment. Her freedom from the other side gave me permission to be free as well.

The 20-minute sitting with Pam was so freeing for me. She offered me a gift of healing that couldn't have been done any other way. No amount of grief therapy could do what she just did. And then, as a cherry on top of the cake, she also offered to teach me how to do this too. Pam was a huge gift from God that day. She demonstrated a way of healing I didn't realise had so much power. Just like that, she opened a door for me. She also became one of my friends and still is to this day.

The Arthur Findlay College

September, 2015

After a month of attending Cowichan Spiritualist Church in Duncan, I started hearing more about the Arthur Findlay College of Psychic Science. At this place in England, Spiritualist mediums go to study Spiritualism, evidential mediumship, trance mediumship, spiritual healing and spirit art. It was well known worldwide and had been operating for many years (since 1964). I had to go. I didn't know how I'd go, but every time I was at a service and heard a medium talk about their experience there, I'd say to myself, *"I am going to go to this place."*

It didn't take long after saying that a surprise inheritance came through from my grandmother (6 months after she passed) that was specifically asked to be used for education. Now, it didn't say what kind of education, but after that reading with Reverend Malcolm Gloster, I knew in my heart that my grandmother would love it if I used that money to attend the college in England. And I did, seven times over eight years. (It would have been more if it wasn't for the pandemic and lockdown). I made sure I made good use of the money she gifted me.

The first time I attended the college in September 2015, I felt a sense of home away from home as soon as I stepped into the building. Like I had stepped into an alternate world and was thrilled every minute of being there. On the first full day, I was partnered with a lady who brought through my grandmother. She shared some evidence of who she was to let me know that it was her. It was my mom's mom, she had passed within the year, had heart problems, was the matriarch of the family, was European, etc. At the end of the message of bringing her through, she said, *"Your grandmother is so proud of you for coming here. So much so that she wants to give you a bouquet of roses. Wait… Orange roses."*

I smiled. How sweet, I thought, that my grandmother wanted to give me a gift of roses. She preferred yellow roses, but close enough, I thought. I thanked the medium, and then we carried on to where we switched, and I gave her a reading. I thought the message from this lady was lovely but didn't overthink it.

The following day, as I was getting ready for classes at 8:30 am, there was a knock on my bedroom door. I was brushing my teeth and hoping my roommate would answer the door, but when I turned around, she was also busy on her laptop sending emails. So, I spat out my toothpaste, wiped my mouth and answered the door still in my pajamas. Standing at the door was a woman holding a bouquet of orange roses.

"Hi," she said nervously.

I said hi back and asked her what she needed.

She told me she was from London and was late starting the course this week due to work but was leaving her office late last night. As she was packing up, she thought it would be such a disappointment to leave this fresh bouquet of orange roses on her work desk. She then thought she would take them to the Arthur Findlay College, run up to the second floor of the Manor, knock on a random door, and gift these orange roses to the first person who opened the door to her.

Everything in that moment felt surreal. Could this actually be happening? This random woman, with a random thought, coming to a random door to deliver random flowers was not random at all. My grandmother was influencing her, passing on a bouquet of orange roses to let her granddaughter know how proud she was of her for following through on her dream.

I graciously took the flowers and shut the door. When reality sank in of what was happening, I found the lady who dropped them off later in the day, thanked her repeatedly and told her of my reading yesterday.

Sometimes, we think we are being random, then we realise there is nothing random about life at all. You can't make this stuff up.

The Power

"Let yourself be silently drawn by the strange pull of what you really love. It will not lead you astray." - Rumi

September, 2015

While at Arthur Findlay College, we were sent to the Sanctuary (chapel) on the first morning to do our class. As I walked in, I was taken by the beautiful royal blue carpets, stained glass windows, and gold trim. I sat in one of the gold velvety chairs in the front row, and our tutor led us through a Sitting in The Power exercise, which I will shortly introduce to you. I placed my hands on my lap and closed my eyes with a smile. I lost track of his words as he led us through the exercise. My arms fell to my side, my spine started to stand up straight, and my chest began to open as my chin rose. The sun beamed from the stained glass window and shone directly over my heart. My hands started to move as they rose slowly. I felt this force field of energy move through me and strengthen me. I wanted to stand up as I felt like I would burst with the energy moving through me.

A memory quickly came to me of when I was 14 and went to a Christian church with Mary. She took us to "The Place", a youth group Sunday evening service filled with songs and devotion. I didn't grow up in a household that practiced any religion, so going to something like this was unfamiliar. Something similar happened to me at The Place, a stained glass window there caused light to beam right into the physical location of my heart. I stood up, raised my hands in the air, and sang along to the beautiful gospel music because it felt so good. I had a moment, a prophetic feeling. At that moment in The Place, I remember hearing a voice whisper in my right ear, *"You will be a minister one day."*

"Impossible", I replied under my breath.

"Maybe....," the voice echoed, disappearing as quickly as it came in.

As I brought my focus back to the classroom at the Arthur Findlay College, I noticed my arms starting to rise again. The tutor gently guided us out of the meditation and asked us what we felt. I looked at him as he looked at me, and I said, *"It moved me"*. He smiled, *"That's the power, my dear."*

The power is God's force that moves through you. This power can move through you when you get out of the way enough. As a medium, the power is the source in which you can connect to all that is. It rides in on the vibration of love, and when you open yourself to that power in a high vibrational state of love, Spirit can meet you. The more you can move out of your mind and into your feeling centre, the stronger it can become. Mediumship is a process of letting go and getting out of the way so Spirit can come through. Some people are better at getting out of the way than others, while some take time to practice. That is why, when you hear a medium being asked about the secret to being a good medium, nine times out of ten, they will tell you, "*You need to learn how to sit and develop that power within you*".

As you sit, let go and vibrate in that state of love so Spirit can move through you. It can develop you and envelop you in that oneness. It will positively transform your life if used for the highest and best good. There is only one power in the universe, and how you choose to use it is entirely up to you. Will you use it to create more joy, love and grace in this world? Choosing to see the good in and contribute from a place of loving service? Or will you choose to focus your energy on what's evil, greedy, dark, and selfish (there is no authentic spirit communication from here, it is just an untrained medium). What you put your attention on grows, and your thoughts create your reality. You are a co-creator in this universe. You are the human, the avatar. You are the one here on Earth representing all the unseen forces in the unseen world. For every person, there is an uncountable amount of unseen support, always evolving, growing and expanding with you as you let it in. The power within you is a part of you, and when you learn to use that power from a place of love, it will enrich your life and all those you touch. You will never know the extent of your ripple effect on humanity from your limited lens in this life. But know it contributes to the whole. You are placed here for a reason in this life and at this time. Your energy has a place here in humanity. Choose to make your contribution with love.

Practice Sitting In The Power

Find a spot to sit quietly, undisturbed. Sit in a chair, upright, with your feet flat on the ground.

Keep your back straight and your hands on your lap. If it's hard for you to sit still comfortably, I recommend walking or doing some movement before sitting. This can still the body so you don't feel restless. Or you can shake it out by physically shaking your hands or feet.

Take a few deep breaths as you begin to slow your breath and bring your awareness out of your head and into your heart.

As you slow your breathing and take your awareness away from your mind and into your body, let your eyes naturally begin to softly close when they are ready.

As you breathe, please bring your awareness into that place within you that feels powerful and strong. This may be your heart, below your rib cage, or your stomach. Just trace your thoughts into that place within you that you know is your strength.

Now that you are in touch with that strong place within you imagine a flame flickering right there. Start to breathe in that light with your breath.

With each breath, I want you to feel, see and intend to grow that light bigger and brighter.

Take your time breathing into that light, letting it naturally expand with each breath.

Fill your whole inside with light, then when full, let it spill into your auric field. (Your energy body around your physical being). Let your power begin to surround you with light, now energising and growing within and around you.

Keep growing the power as it touches the edges of your room. Feel the edges and fill the room with your power as it rises in the vibration of love and positivity.

Now, keep breathing and expand your power even bigger. We are connecting you with all of life. The trees, the water, the plants, the animals. All of humanity. Keep expanding your light as you connect with all that is. Become one with consciousness and creator.

Feel the strength in this power. It may even begin to sit you up straight. It gives you a sense of confidence. A power bigger than you. Let it feed you. Let it recharge your batteries, ignite your light and fill you with all the energy you need.

Now sit in this power, put a little smile on your face and rest in it.

When you are learning to sit in the power, you may hold this for a few minutes. The practice is to hold your focus and extend your sitting longer each week. (Kind of like practicing running. You don't run 10km to start, you start with a km, then warm up, lengthening over time.) To sit 15 minutes in the power a day completely undisturbed can dramatically change your life.

Those who work in mediumship often or full time may require more time. I prefer 30 minutes, sometimes more, to keep my power source strong because it just feels good. But everyone's got an opinion about how long or not. Check-in with your body, we are all unique and have different needs. After a while, it starts to feel so good that you will cherish this time, wanting to sit longer and longer, helping you become refreshed, renewed, and even physically better and mentally happier.

When you connect with the power, you strengthen yourself, get out of the mind, recharge your batteries, and connect with all that is.

Some sit in the power with the intention of connecting to Spirit. I recommend learning to sit in the power of stillness first. Learn to move thoughts aside and practice getting out of the way. This will strengthen your mediumship so information can come to you in a clear channel. (Like a clear radio channel instead of being dialled into multiple stations at once).

Also, do not sit in the power to get somewhere. You are practising emptying so you can be filled with the divine presence, not to answer all your spiritual questions. After sitting, those answers may come to you later as you learn to get out of the way. You will notice answers appear in your waking state. Let sitting in the power be a time for you and the God of your own understanding.

To be a medium, you must have a good relationship with the divine source. You cannot grow beyond your own capacity to be a spiritual medium without touching something bigger than you. To keep God out of mediumship is like keeping emotion out of a relationship, it won't get you far and it will stay dry, disconnected and flat. Get to know the presence of all that is and open the door for communication often. The more you develop this relationship and the power within you that connects you to all that life is, the stronger you will become in yourself. In reflection, your mediumship will expand, too.

The Difference Between Sitting In The Power & Meditation

When developing your ability to connect to the other side, it's important to learn how to sit in the power. This is different from a meditation practice. When meditating, you are learning to find a balance between your mind, body, and soul. You go inward, emptying and/or creating a focus on a mantra or affirmation. It's about becoming present. When practising sitting in the power, you are expanding your energy out. You are building the power (life force energy) within you, expanding it into your being, your aura and into the universe. You become one with all that is and grow spiritually in a way that connects you to your spirit team and loved ones in spirit, as well as re-charging your batteries so you can sustain a connection with spirit longer over time. It is a practice of learning to blend your power with the power ~ the greater energy of all that is.

While learning to sit in the power, you become still. You move your awareness to that place of strength within your being that you connected to in the previous exercise, expanding your energy. As you become stronger in the power, your body will become very still when sitting. A blending will begin to take place—a feeling you are being wrapped in the divine's energy. Of course, every person's experience will be unique. But when sharing with friends and students, there are some common experiences I notice people have:

- A feeling of connection, like you are being wrapped in a warm, energetic blanket.
- A sense of comfort, like you are being held.
- A shift in temperature ~ a cool breeze at your feet or a flush of warmth around your face. Or you may feel energy moving around you or even a cobweb feeling, like energy is moving around your face and body. It's like the subtle feeling of hair or cobwebs moving over you (in the most loving way possible).

In this, finding stillness in your body over time, you will start to feel a blending begin to happen as if a warmth of energy is beginning to wrap around you from the divine.

The more still you can become within the power, the more your guides and spirit team can develop your abilities to connect. So much of your unfoldment will be invisible as the spirit world weaves within your very being. As you sit in stillness, you learn to get out of the way, allowing Spirit to draw close to you and sustain a deeper connection with the non-physical world.

Imagine you're going to a practitioner for a treatment like acupuncture. Imagine if you were constantly moving and talking. The practitioner would not be able to put the needles in you. The more you move around, the harder it will be to get close to you. Only when you sit still and relax will the practitioner be able to get close and help you. Like most things in life, you need to be present and still in order for someone to help you physically. This helps me when I picture the spirit world coming and drawing close to me. The more I allow, unwind and open, the more they can come and influence me. Use your power of intention to draw in what is needed. Sometimes, you may ask for assistance with health, healing and personal growth. Take your questions to the divine and ask them to take your burdens while their presence moves through you. Learning to trust the connection and evolve in this will be your greatest tool and asset for mediumistic growth and development.

The Nameless One

"There are no rules of worship. He will hear the voice of every heart that is sincere." – Rumi

I am surprised by how often I have clients who come to see me to connect with loved ones in spirit who are open to the experience, open to their loved ones coming through and are quite easy to work with, but later in the reading or afterwards, they will share with me that they don't believe in God. Now I understand what they are saying- that they don't believe in organised religion or a man in the sky with a beard judging you for your sins. Still, I find it baffling that they can believe in communication with the afterlife but not believe in a higher power.

I have even experienced this with students who have come to classes to learn mediumship and psychic development but will reach a point in their training that they will admit to me that they don't believe in a creator. In these situations, I get very curious about what led them to this point, what opened them to this work and their sensitivity without a feeling of spirit guidance around them. I have heard people share that they believe in quantum energy, the universe, manifesting, the law of attraction, and magnetism but think of it more like a computer. But I am curious to know what they think exists beyond that.

When Mary died, I spent an afternoon with her mother. We went for coffee and drove around Cook Street Village in Victoria, B.C. Mary's mom could tell that the death of her daughter had shaken me to the core, and from her death, my life path had changed. She asked me what I felt called to do with my life now. The answer came to me quickly and from within. I wanted to help people find God.

Since then, my greatest passion has been leading people to find their higher power. After leaving hairdressing and getting my business off the ground as a healer and tarot reader, I worked part-time in a live-in drug and rehabilitation treatment centre in Cowichan, B.C. I wanted to help recovering alcoholics and addicts find a higher power, something beyond them, to restore them to sanity. Lucky for me, I got to go to countless First Nations Sweat Lodge ceremonies led by our community elders as support staff to reconnect patients with their culture and for others to remember who they are. I witnessed true miracles. Seeing the light turn on for someone after abandoning themselves through addiction was life-changing for them and magnificent to witness.

It really doesn't matter what you call it, as our creator is the nameless one. There are no words, no way of explaining what it is that the presence truly is. But as a medium, it is important you explore what it is and means to you.

Mediumship without belief in a higher power will only get you so far. It will leave your work soulless and dry, but who you are beyond that is an intimate journey within yourself, as you will have to find what that power greater than you is, the power that is already within you.

God, creator, the presence, eternal love, Spirit, infinite intelligence - it really does not matter what name you call it. What matters is developing a personal relationship with the unseen world. The creator will speak to you as you open yourself to this connection, which will be for you individually.

Please take some time to find a connection with your higher power in a way that resonates. Going beyond the limitations of the mind allows you to reach for more of what this life can truly offer you, as the power within you is also of you. When you connect with it, it will deepen and enrich your life indefinitely.

Exercise:

1) When you hear the word God, what do you notice? Does it feel heavy, light and freeing, or constricting? Feel it in your body and breathe into it. Acknowledge it without needing to fix it.

2) Bring your attention to the seat of strength and light you found in your body in the previous exercise. This is where

you will find God. Not out there in the stars, although God is there too, but within your own being. Rest in your being. Throughout the day, take some time to be present with this, your hand on your heart, to begin to affirm this if it is new to you.

3) Reflect on things that have happened to you that you cannot explain. Are there situations in your life where you have experienced miracles? Can you begin to accept that the source of the miracles is within you?

4) What beliefs about God did you learn earlier in life that no longer serve? Are you ready to let them go to embrace a more empowered version of you supported by God?

Chapter 4: Possibility

~

Seeing Signs Everywhere

"There are only two ways to live your life. One is as though nothing is a miracle. The other is as though everything is a miracle." - Albert Einstein

2016

When I started studying evidential mediumship in England at the Arthur Findlay College, the tutors highly emphasised and trained me on the importance of bringing through the essence of the spirit, sharing their story, and allowing them to express themselves through me. It is not about bringing your shopping list of evidence you need for spirit confirmation at your pleasure, for this actually blocks what may be trying to come through in a reading. You may have a word or name you want the medium to say or a particular item of jewellery to be mentioned. Still, your attachment to hearing specifics can cause you to miss the equally helpful and valid evidence coming through that you may not be expecting. Trust that spirit knows what you need to hear in that moment.

I know the more I try to get something from spirit, the more it's blocked, and the more I let go, the more a reading can flow. I allow spirit to surprise me with their intelligence. Usually, the most open clients or those with no agenda receive more, and those with high expectations could leave disappointed even when I know I have brought through strong evidence. I believe this to be true because when you hang onto something too tightly, it blocks possibility. Spirit is boundless, yet when you try to force an outcome, it shrinks the lens through which it can move.

Names can be like that. When I first started mediumship, I used to get names a lot. Spirit would bring them to me by showing me someone I knew with that name, like an acquaintance I knew, or a character from a movie or TV show with that name. When I'd see an image of a person out of nowhere from a recognisable film, it often meant a name, and usually, it was accurate. As I evolved, I created easier ways and shortcuts to get to the point with spirit communication. This means I'd ask them to bring me evidence in a way I could understand quickly. Instead of sending me all these images, they'd show me someone like my dad, and from there, I could get a great feel for who they were in spirit.

But now and then, Spirit would do something that was so out of the box that the only thing I could do was laugh.

A lady came to visit me at my office for a session. About five minutes before she arrived, I noticed this huge ant on the wall. I placed it in a cup and moved it to the window. I never shut the window, though. My client showed up, and we started her reading. About halfway through her reading, we started getting into signs from loved ones, and she was saying to me that she felt she could make a sign out of anything. This makes me laugh, as I know what that's like. You see a hummingbird fly past you and start crying, saying that's your grandma. At the same time, someone else who may have a completely different relationship with life would see just a hummingbird or not even see it at all. But anyway, we continued, and I started bringing through a loved one in spirit for her. She confirmed the information brought through of who he was, and suddenly, I noticed that huge ant on the wall again. I got distracted and made a quick reference to it, hoping she wasn't creeped out by it. I told her I had put it out before she arrived, but this ant on the wall was again here. She started laughing uncontrollably. What was so funny? Usually, I could stay focused on my readings, I rarely get pulled and distracted, but this was bugging me. She laughed and shared with me. *"Well, the man you are bringing through in spirit, his name was Anton. Like the ant-on-the-wall!"*

Ha, I thought. Even when I think I'm not, I'm still connected. We are all so connected. It's so interwoven that we can't get it wrong. My client made a good point that day: you can choose to see a sign in anything, and your world will become quite magical and creative. The more you appreciate and show awe in the wonder of this creation, the more you are giving spirit to work with. What you appreciate, appreciates. For those who are in gratitude, things multiply. I loved that that happened for her, and she taught me a valuable lesson that day: if I choose to see the world as magical, I will be forever entertained as we each create the world we see. I wonder how often things like this happen and we don't even notice.

The Clock Story

I have a clock that I inherited after my grandmother died in October 2014. It was the only thing I asked for out of her house while the family was cleaning it out. It was a handmade clock made of pottery with a little clay mouse in the corner. When I was a child, I used to stare up at this clock in awe. It hung in the kitchen of my grandparents' house. It brought me many great memories of my grandmother's cooking and waiting with my grandfather to see the clock hit a certain time before we ate. We would wait patiently for our food and sit together, watching the clock tick on the wall.

When I took this clock, I brought it into my healing room. It had an insanely loud clock sound. It was so loud that my clients sometimes commented on it when sitting in my room with me. Funny enough, though, the moment we'd start the reading, it was like the sound of the clock would go away. This clock was about 25 years old when I inherited it, and I treated it well. I hung it up nicely across from me, displaying it on the wall so people could see.

In the Spring of 2016, the clock stopped working. I tried changing the batteries and adjusting the back end. Sad and disappointed, I had to accept that the clock was now broken.

That there was nothing I could do to fix it. Many of my friends and family members looked at it, all saying the same: there was no real good reason why it stopped working, but putting new batteries in wasn't fixing it. It was an old clock, so I accepted it was done but never took it off the wall. It was permanent at the time of 10. I kept it on the wall hanging there on display for three months, no ticking, the time completely off, but I didn't have the heart to take it down. I laughed when clients got confused with the time, letting them know I had sentimental value to the clock, and it brought me joy just being there, even if it didn't work anymore. I thought, eventually, it would get old, and I would take it off the wall. I just wasn't there yet... until one day in July 2016.

I had a client come that day with her mother for a reading. It was at 10 am, and, when I ran up the stairs to start setting up the room, I heard this ticking sound as I entered the room. The clock was ticking; the clock had changed the time to 10:40 am. It had been working for about forty minutes, and there was no explanation for why or how this phenomenon happened. I wasn't too convinced it would stay working, but I happily adjusted the time to 9:50 am and waited for my clients to show up.

The mother and daughter sat before me and asked if they could have a mediumship reading. I said yes and moved my tarot cards aside. As I closed my eyes, I connected energetically with each of them and then started to call in their loved ones in spirit under my breath. Very quickly, a presence stood directly behind me on my right side. I was aware of a grandfather/father standing behind me. They confirmed it was her father, her grandfather. He showed me an image of him working in a shop, like a garage. They confirmed that, yes, he did this. All of a sudden, I started to notice the sound of the clock ticking on the wall incredibly loud. It was so loud that I couldn't stay focused and was quite distracted; I thought I was being pulled out of the reading. I opened my eyes and looked directly at the clock on the wall, watching it tick and the time continuing to change. Suddenly, as I looked at the clock on the wall, a vision appeared over it. I saw the man in his shop with all these clocks on his workbench. He was there with his wrench and screwdriver and showed me him tinkering on them.

"Your father/grandfather is showing me that he liked to fix clocks," I said, a little surprised.

They started laughing and said, *"YES! He fixed all our clocks!"*

I couldn't believe what was happening. I continued sharing what he was showing me, about how he was very passionate about this, and that he would buy clocks, fix them, and give them away to the family and friends. They laughed as I shared this as, apparently, he was really known for this.

After the reading, I shared about my clock and how it had started working again for the first time in 3 months when I came into the room. They listened and laughed a bit, but I am not quite sure they believed me. I wasn't even sure I believed it.

To this date, 2024, the clock is still working and has never skipped a beat. I have not had any problems with it again and will keep using this clock until it falls off the wall. It was such good confirmation for me that not only do your loved ones in spirit choose to come through, but they also take the opportunity to help out where they can, too, where their service is needed.

Asking For A Sign From A Loved One In Spirit

When asking for a sign, it's important to set your intention first. Your intention is pivotal in asking, as it will shift your outcome. Also, signs can be used to let us know that our loved ones are around us, but they are also there to teach us to ask for help and confirmation.

When asking for a sign from a loved one in spirit, you may be emotionally charged, so it may not be obvious if you receive one. You have to remember that your loved ones in spirit are always around you. They are always watching over you, and quite often, they will do things to catch your attention, but you may not be aware that this is a sign, or your mind will override it and not notice. When in deep grief, this is incredibly easy to do. Grief puts you in a mental fog, and it's hard to see anything. When speaking with clients about this, they will tell me they always ask for signs but don't always receive them. When I mention a few things, they will often say, *"That's a sign?"*

Open your mind, and learn to become marvelled by the world we live in. All is connected. There is perfect order in this universe, and alignment happens when your thoughts, actions and intentions come together.

Declare you want a sign from a specific loved one in spirit. I always say it out loud, as the power of a spoken word is powerful. *"Hi [name], I am asking for a sign from you today. Please make it obvious so that I know you are around me. I give you full creative control of the sign, but please help me see it. I promise I'll pay attention."*

Let go. After you have asked for a sign, let go completely and continue your day. Try not to obsess about it, looking around at everything around you will only get you in the way. When we are not thinking about it, things come to us because we let go of control. When you let go, the divine can come in there. Just like how in life, if we are too hyper-focused on something, we push it away. It would be best to learn to become light about it, as light energy is a higher vibration and lets things in faster.

When a sign does come to you, big or small, say thank you. Learn to let those be your words to the creator. *Thank you for this day, this life, this car I have, the roof over my head, and the people around me.* Gratitude is a sure way to raise your frequency and open your eyes to see what you could not see before. Gratitude for Spirit and life also helps you become a magnet. The more you show your gratitude to Spirit for signs, the more often synchronicity happens.

Signs are a way to help us feel connected. To stay in the flow as well as be in harmony with life. Life is better when you are balanced and aligned with all that is. If you are not feeling synchronicity and guided pulls, this may be an indication that you may want to shift directions. Or to ask for Spirit to put you on a good path and lead you.

After a while, and after many received signs, you may start to feel as if you are connected to all of life. You will start to notice and appreciate every action, instant, or shift around you and pay attention. As you will begin to see, you are in this life, a part of this life, and all that is happening around you is in harmony with the universe. When you get to this place, signs may not fall out of the sky for you to get your attention like they used to. This does not mean that you are less connected. It means that you are more connected, and the spirit world doesn't have to try so hard to knock you over the head to tell you they are there. You will recognise it as just part of life and synchronicity. You will feel it and have a connection to all of life.

When I first started mediumship, I would receive mind-blowing and very obvious signs, such as the clock story and the knocking that I used to hear in our house. I don't receive quite as many blaring signs as often now because I have a deeper trust, and so I have come into relationship with Spirit more easily, and it feels more flowing. The communication is more subtle but still profound, it's like I am living in synchronicity but not as shocked each time something happens. They don't have to work as hard to get my attention, but it's a more harmonious exchange. The connection is a part of me.

The Power of Intention

*"In the universe there is an immeasurable,
indescribable force which shamans call intent, and
absolutely everything that exists in the entire cosmos is
attached to intent by a connecting link."* - Carlos Castaneda

Everything is intention: the work you do, the way you do it, how you do it, and the energy you bring through while doing it. Intention is the starting point to joining with Spirit and bringing forth what gets created from there. As a medium, you have to become incredibly disciplined in working with energy and the power of intention. You must understand you are working with a power greater than you, and your intention dictates the direction it goes. There is only one power in the universe, how you use it is up to you.

Becoming a medium, you start to recognise the limitless power you are working with. As you grow in your abilities, your most important asset is keeping your mind expanded and open, and doing this work for the highest and best good. Your intention for mediumship allows you to bring through new information, to bring through key pieces that are important, as well as doing this work for a higher purpose than yourself.

People often tell me they fear mediumship because they do not know what they are opening up to. While I understand this, I also know that if you set good intentions before you do any spirit work, you will be met with good intentions because energy flows where your mind goes. It works best when you become grounded and disciplined in what you are doing. From the way you open up, who you choose to connect with, as well as your purpose for doing it. Your intention is your silent prayer. It moves you in the direction to unfold from there - what you put your intention on grows. You are a co-creator in this creation—every single time.

A huge part of mediumship development is sitting in the power. This builds your power so you can connect to spirit, but your intention allows you to align your thoughts, power and action to what will manifest. Mediumship is an active power. It's in the moment, fluid and harmonious between you, the spirit world and the person receiving the communication. The three of you will join in union, and with alignment and staying focused and in the flow, miracles can occur. All mediumship is done in the vibration of love. That is the address of the spirit world.

As you grow in confidence, you will notice your power of intention will quicken. You will start to open up and align your thoughts. Quite quickly, you will be met halfway. Spirit is quick to correspond once you know what you are doing and understand energy. If it is not working, it could mean you are too crowded in your head, possibly not grounded or clear-minded, splitting your intention (meaning not focusing and being indecisive) and do not have enough power to hold the connection or belief in self.

This work is not necessarily hard to do. It does not require hours of meditation, years of research, a PhD or hours of trying to get there mentally. Actually, it's quite the opposite. It's all about alignment and openness in your energy. To some people, it may come more easily and naturally, while to others, it may take time to get out of their heads or believe in themselves. Whatever it is, it will be your own experience, and mediumship will always meet you where you are, showing you the next step in your soul's growth.

So, before you jump into mediumship, make sure you ask yourself…

What is my intention?
Why am I doing this?
Who am I asking to connect to?
What energy do I want to bring through in this communication?

As an example, this is a process I go through before a reading…

Why am I doing this? To bring healing and comfort to those who have lost a loved one. To give them the same peace and awakening it gave me when I first went through this. It altered and changed the course of my life, and I never looked at death the same again.

Who am I connecting to? To loved ones in spirit that are relevant to the person receiving this communication.

What energy do I want to bring through in this communication? I want it to be soulful, meaningful, evidential (undeniable that it's them), graceful, flowing and bring through exactly what is needed.

The Power of Prayer

"For prayer is nothing else than being on terms of friendship with God." - Saint Teresa of Avila

If you don't want to cause people harm, you pray to do good in the world. If you don't want to become overwhelmed with spirits visiting you in your waking life, you pray for a gentle opening and visiting hours. Pray for miracles, to be a vessel for the creator to work through you in ways beyond your imagination, to help you get out of the way.

Prayer is how you connect with something bigger than you. It's communication with the divine. In order to be a spiritual medium, I encourage daily prayer as the way of staying in constant contact with the divine.

I often hear people say they don't pray because it's weird. They aren't religious or don't want to sound stupid. But what really is true prayer? It is to learn how to be in union and conversation with Source. There is no mediumship where Spirit isn't present. It would be best if you learned how to take ownership of what you are doing and the power you are working with. Prayer is your way to be in communion and asking for help beyond you. Prayer is how you go beyond what is possible in the physical realm and reach out to Spirit to work with you and help. As you grow in your development, you will feel less out of control in your abilities and more grounded in your connection to Spirit. Realising you are co-creating what you let into your world. To pray is the greatest gift you can give back to yourself, as it will open and bless your world with grace.

So often, I hear about mediums feeling like they are under so much pressure, as if they are the ones doing all the work. Yes, you can decide when and where you offer your service and how you prepare your vessel, but Spirit is who you work for. To pray is to go beyond the physical realm, opening you up to the intelligence beyond you. Mediumship is not about looking clever or impressive, it's not even about you. It is about being a bridge between worlds, giving messages from spirit to those who need it.

At any moment, if you don't like how things are feeling or where things are going or feel unsafe, you use prayer to ask for the divine to help you. To take away the dark thoughts, to hand over what doesn't serve you, to put you on the right path and take over from here. It's about surrendering to the unknown but using the power of your words to keep yourself on the right path. So often, I get asked in readings for people to let them know if they are on the right path. At any moment, you can ask the creator, *"Put me on the right path. Place me where you need me"*. This takes the pressure off of trying to do everything yourself and wondering if everything will work out okay. You ask for help and guidance, and it will shift your world.

Mediumship development is realising you have to take ownership of your life and what you let into your mind. You learn quickly that your thoughts create an outcome and can quickly pull you down or direct you back up. As you develop your abilities, things may begin to get more intense. As you own your power more, you become a more conscious creator. You learn to be in connection with the divine more frequently, allowing yourself to be a conduit for spirit as well as realising the direction your energy goes is in alignment with your thoughts. The saying goes, *"Worrying is praying for what you don't want"*. Or, if you don't want your world filled with darkness, don't put your attention on it and stop watching violence and serial killers on TV. Place your thoughts in the direction you want to go and learn to discipline your mind. Prayer is a fast way to align yourself with the life you want so things can become simplified, graceful, soulful and light.

Prayer doesn't have to be formal. It can literally be, *"Help me!"* Of course, I recommend using prayer sacredly, as it's not like demanding attention from a friend. But it is a way to become reverent with the divine. *"Creator, please help me; thank you!"* would be a richer way of saying it. But know you create your relationship in a way that makes sense to you. When you do this, you are developing a direct connection with your divine family, so you speak to the creator in ways you would want to be spoken to. Know that when you come with humility, it will always be met with grace.

Talk to Spirit often, and let your spirit team become your best friends. As with any relationship you put effort into, the more you communicate and stay in touch, the stronger and more trusting the relationship becomes. The more you learn to hand things over, the more in flow you will become. Inspired action comes when you take the burden off of you and place it back in the hands of the divine. As you lift that load off, trying to carry what's not yours to hold or what makes you feel out of control, a thought or inspiration may come through that will shift and direct your life in ways you may have never considered. Prayer is about union with the divine.

Guides

When you first start awakening to mediumship, sometimes there is an urgency to meet the guides in some kind of form. Now, of course, your guides may come to you in human form, but it is also very common for them to come as just energy. Think of it as a collective consciousness wrapping their love all around you. Over time, they may take form, as they will come to you as you as you feel comfortable seeing them. Remember, in spirit, we are not physical beings but energy and light, but our human minds can relate to things that make sense and feel welcome to us. So, often, spirit guides take form and names so they can relate to us.

Please do not rush to try and figure out who they are, what their names are, what they are here to teach you, etc. You will get in your head and lose connection fast. Let them come to you as you invite them in. Let them unfold you and let this be a relationship that develops over time. Each person will have their own time frame for development. There is no rush or no time limit. Allowing Spirit to blend with your spirit is most important in these early stages. This develops the bond, the relationship and continuous growth can happen in your mediumship unfoldment from here.

Think of it as a meeting with your team. You become an empty vessel, and they come when they are called to develop and influence you in the power. Place no agenda on them, as they are here to guide you, not run your life. As you learn to let them draw close to you, put out an offering or intention. They are always there and willing to teach you as you learn to listen and feel them.

Different guides will come to you based on your interests. This means that depending on what you are going through in life, as well as what you may take on, different bands of energy will wrap around you to support you in that development. An example is when you take on a new creative project, inspiration will come from guides that can support you with this in such things as music, art, and writing. The stronger you become in something and let go into it, the more your spirit team can help and influence you in that way. You see this with athletes when they get so in the flow of their sport that it's as if something comes through them. Or musicians when they find the frequency in the music and experience pure bliss. Or an artist who loses complete track of time and feels like they were in a trance. It's because spirit has taken over. Over time, your guides and spirit team will become your most cherished friends. The more you practice a craft or something that calls your attention and let go into it, the more your guides can influence you. Just like how when you loosen up before doing something important (like public speaking or playing a game) and the more relaxed you are, the more natural it will unfold within you.

Exercise To Meet Your Guides

Before doing this exercise, please make sure you have practiced Sitting in The Power (chapter 3) first.

Begin by sitting comfortably in your chair. I prefer dim lights or the dark, but this is a personal preference. I find sitting in the dark takes away physical distractions and takes me deeper, but do what makes you comfortable. Sitting in an undisturbed closed room also contains the energy better.

If you are restless, give your limbs a shake before sitting down. I do this by stretching, and I wait until the end of the day when I am more relaxed to practice this, or first thing in the morning before I do anything. Sometimes, going for a workout first or walking helps me energetically rest my body.

So often when I hear about people who can't meditate, it's because they are trying to do it while jacked on caffeine or in the middle of the afternoon when they have ten other things they are meant to be doing. Find time for your practice; this is just for you. It's a sacred act and should be a time you look forward to in the day.

Rest your hands on your lap and take a few deep breaths as you begin to rest your body. Bring your awareness into your chest while moving your mind from your head to your heart. Naturally, your eyes will begin to soften and close when they are ready. Take some breaths from your heart centre, as breathing slows you down and helps you move into a more peaceful state.

Breathe into the power as you start to expand your energy. Feel the love begin to build from within. Let it raise your vibration naturally and connect you with all that is. Take your time getting into this flow. Breathing in and out until it becomes natural, like a wave flowing in the ocean. Feel all that is around you, feeling that state of bliss as your energy increases in sensitivity.

When you feel balanced in this flow, begin to set your intention for your spirit team to come to be with you. Invite them to come close. Let them wrap you with their loving energy. Say this within your mind and gently take note of what begins to shift and transpire within and around you.

The first few times you do this, don't expect huge results. To feel your guides is a feeling. You are developing your power to feel more of the non-physical world around you. You are developing a relationship with your spirit team by doing this. You are connecting on that vibration of love where you can meet them. This may be an emotional process as you begin to welcome in the love of their divine presence.
Sit in this power of the presence of your guides for as long as you need. Extend your time longer weekly, letting them

help you develop your spirit (starting with 5 minutes and working your way up to 15 minutes is more than enough, or extend to 30 minutes if you want). The longer you can sit in their presence, the more they can influence you. It is important in mediumship development that you take the time to let them blend with your soul.

When you are finished, begin to pull your energy back to you, as if you are tucking in your energetic wings. Once you feel grounded and centred, open your eyes and thank your guides for their presence all around you.

Practice inviting your guides to help and influence you whenever possible.

Writing a paper?

Invite your guides to help you.

Going for a walk?

Invite your guides to come with you and inspire you.

Working on a research project?

Ask your guides to direct you to what you need to look at.

Let your relationship build over time, knowing that they are always there, just waiting for the invitation. The more you call them in, the closer they will become.

Automatic Writing

Automatic writing can be a powerful tool, not only to get to know yourself deeper, but it's also a way for you to connect with your spirit team. Automatic writing is a kind of mediumship development where you learn to let go and let your pen flow on paper. It's about getting out of your head and allowing your pen to flow with what is being written through you. Based on your preparation for getting into automatic writing as well as your intention, your results may vary.

To start, I want you to take a pen and a sheet of paper and place them right next to you. I want you to practice Sitting in the Power (chapter 3) and Meet Your Guides (chapter 4) before practicing automatic writing. I want to ensure you can sense the presence of spirit around you first. Give yourself time to feel that connection. Automatic writing is a great next step when you feel ready to take this relationship deeper.

You may play background music to soothe you as you prepare for your writing exercise. Binaural beats are my favourite. Go to YouTube or another music app and type in *528 hertz and 432 hertz*. Listen to sound frequencies that put you in the zone.

Once you feel that strong connection with your guides all around you, I want you to take the pen in your hand and put the paper in front of you. Wait until you almost feel a pulse, as if something is starting to get you to take the next step (like inspired action). At the top of your page, I want you to write:

Dear (your first name),

Now, let your pen flow through your hand and start writing. Do not edit what is being written. Do not stop and re-read what is being written as you write it (this is when we get nosey, and it prevents us from getting in the flow). Let your handwriting shift. You may write really fast, or you may notice as an observation that you write a little bit differently when you write this way. Let the page fill with this note from spirit. When you feel the writing naturally coming to a close, sign it with the name of the person who wrote it. This may look like *"Your spirit guide, Bob"* or *"Collective consciousness"*, etc..... Trust that whatever is written is needed.

After you put your pen down, glance at what you have written. Notice the shift in the writing. Did this sound like something you'd say or write? Or does it feel different? Is it uplifting or critical? (Our minds are critical, but messages from spirit are empowering and always kind). Pay attention to the way it is written to you. One thing to always keep in mind is when spirit is writing, it's always going to be uplifting, motivating and inspiring. The mind loves to critique, put down, fix and tell you what's wrong with you.

Or, the opposite with grandiose messages like, *"You are the only person in the world who can do this. You are the chosen one. You have the highest abilities of psychic powers we've ever seen."* Take notice, for this is your mind getting in there and the ego loves to inflate, divide and conquer. This is NOT spirit. You may notice the written letter starts uplifting and positive, and then you can assess where the mind got in and took over by being overly critical or self-aggrandising. Use your discernment and learn the difference. Observe your work, notice what feels like you and get to know what feels like spirit.

Practice this daily for one month. Notice how your pen begins to loosen. Notice how it strengthens over time, and observe your automatic writing. Pay attention to the differences in your writing over time. It's nice to add intentions to your letters, too. One day, ask what you most need to know or your deepest longing. Ask for guidance on a specific subject in your life. Or even ask who is writing with you and how they support you from Spirit.

Many authors do automatic writing when they are writing books. Over time, when someone practices writing as a skill, they hit a point where they just let go, and their fingers move, typing out thesis papers, journalism articles or books close to the author's heart. To write is a very powerful way to express yourself creatively. When you can invite spirit to work through you and be a part of this process, it will shift magically, gliding off the page. It just takes your willingness to get out of the way and discipline to practice often so you stretch the muscle. Psychic work is about stretching a muscle to open up a new pathway. Otherwise, you will always write the way you write. Until you give permission and practice letting go, then the divine can more easily write through you.

Chapter 5: Alignment

~

Becoming More Sensitive

Before the term medium was used, mediums used to be called "sensitives". This would mean that they used their sensitivity to feel into energy around them and in their environment. When attuned properly, they could use their highly sensitive abilities to tune into the non-physical world, which allowed them to communicate with the dead.

The common thread I encounter when meeting people drawn to the path of mediumship is that they are highly sensitive beings and empaths. Until a point in their life, their sensitivity was probably a survival skill to bear uneasy situations in their home environment, in school or in workplaces. Sensitives have the ability to feel out situations before someone even says something. So, as a survival tactic, sensitivity could be used to avoid confrontation and unease in the environment and to fix people. This could lead to codependency, becoming easily overwhelmed, not being okay until the other person is okay, or even trying to heal people so the sensitive can relax. Again, this could be a coping mechanism, not always operating from one's gifts as a sensitive and empath.

The highly sensitive person, if called to explore their gifts deeper, will greatly benefit from developing healthy boundaries, living a more balanced life and being in touch with nature. When diving into your gifts as a medium, your sensitivity will increase and you become more heightened.

Most of the exercises given to mediums are intended to increase your sensitivity so that you can feel, see, hear, taste, smell, and know senses around you that are not in the physical world. It's to be able to heighten abilities so that you can become stronger in your gift. Sometimes, people forget when developing their mediumship that it is not singled out to this one area of sensitivity but all areas of their life. This causes people to become more emotional, feel more feelings, acknowledge their pain and deal with what comes up. Mediumship will dramatically increase any area of your life where you haven't felt something deeply. It will take you directly there, helping you face aspects of your past, your present and remind you to be there for yourself and ask for help. The unhealthy pattern of the empath is to be there for everyone but not let anyone be there for them, as they are *fine*!

I see potential mediums and healers get stuck when they think they are not strong enough to do the inner inquiry that is calling them. They freak out, get hard on themselves, and continue to shelve their emotions, wondering why their mediumship isn't evolving. Mediumship cannot be placed in a box. You cannot save it for Spiritualist service on Sundays or circle Wednesday nights, but it begins to weave within your whole being. This allows you to shift your relationships, heal your physical self, strengthen the mind, body, soul connection and empower yourself. Once you realise you are not only part of the power but are the power manifested in physical form, you start to realise the responsibility you have on this Earth- that no one is responsible for you but you to change your life for the better. Only you can feel your emotions, others cannot do it for you, or you do not have to do it for them. It's a process of growing up and recognising the maturity that comes with this gift.

When you treat your sensitivity as a gift, you will nurture it, take care of it and honour it accordingly. But if you dismiss it and treat it as a curse, a way to show off, or take from others, you will not ever see the benefits of what love so freely given can do for others in this lifetime. You and the one who sent you have mindfully chosen your life. Perfectly on time, at this moment, in this lifetime. How you choose to live is entirely up to you. When you increase your sensitivity, know that every emotion you feel within allows you to hold that space for another. Your wisdom will pour through you in situations so effortlessly with divine knowing and grace, as nothing is truly healed within until it is freely given away.

Being a medium is a brave path. You will face obstacles, potentially be cut off from circles and parts of society, and could be called a fraud or even dangerous for what you do. All this comes from a place of lack of understanding and fear. But you will stand up anyway because once Spirit has touched your heart in this way, and you have shared it, nothing will ever compare to the love and bliss you will feel of being of service to the divine creator and sharing your gifts with the world.

Personal Integrity

"Where there is great power, there is a great responsibility." - Winston Churchill

Mediumship is a path of service. It is about developing the power within you to become a bridge between worlds and giving the spirit world a voice. You are developing the power so you can understand yourself and be of service to Spirit and share what needs to be communicated. True mediumship is not about self-inflation, but within this service, you will be deeply enriched and spiritually fed. What you give to others will have an effect on you, for being touched by someone's loved one in spirit can be very transformative.

Sometimes, I see people drawn to mediumship because they like the idea of impressing others. It's as if it will give them extra sensory abilities to make them special, stand out and become rich and famous. But spirit doesn't serve egos, and many who claim they are working that way may be good entertainers or like to serve a life of glitz and glam. Not all, of course. Sometimes, Spirit uses people in this way to reach the masses, but it's about being led to where you are being taken instead of trying to obtain popularity. This is about putting Spirit in the front seat and sharing this gift with those around you.

In this power, there is a great responsibility. You must learn to put the focus back on Spirit, learning to become a channel of love and bring through what is being called forth. You may be placed in uncomfortable situations where you will be forced to grow and truly share what you are getting from Spirit despite feeling vulnerable. Also, it will meet you in those places where you are being asked to grow. As you develop your mediumship, you will reach moments where you cannot go deeper in a spirit communication. Those are the moments you are being asked to go deeper within yourself and foster your own personal growth and development.

For instance, you may have a client that you are unable to help, and then something in your life causes you to look deeper within and brings about an opening for you. You may feel called to make some changes in your work or even changing career, and until you have seen it through and taken the leaps yourself, it will be hard to guide someone else through that process. Sometimes Spirit might be giving guidance to your client and you realise that what you are sharing with them is exactly what you need to apply to your own life.

You're expanding so you can overcome those limitations within you. As you awaken, your heart will open, creating stronger connections with people and increasing sensitivity and responsibility for what you do. You are not there to people please, to tell others what they want to hear by psychically pulling you in, but to share what truly needs to be said. All messages should be, of course, encouraging messages of hope, healing and transformation. In this, your personal power will increase, not because of inflation of self, but because the service you give to others will give back to you tenfold.

Mediumship is a calling from within, and you are there to represent the spirit world. If you are drawn to this path, listen. You will be guided to the right people and places to help you develop. Your life will change, and you may want to be further ahead than where you are. But be patient, listen to the signs and choose to do this work with integrity and honour. The more you give to Spirit from a place of your heart, the more the Spirit world will give back to you in love and compassion. Mediumship is an ability that can be learned to an extent, but being a spiritual medium is a spiritual gift as you cannot make a spark within someone. Know that the creator put mediumship before you as a path to awaken. All you have to do is follow the next step.

And if you don't listen, the signs may get louder!

Psychic Versus Mediumship

It's important to know the different ways to do readings, as well as be disciplined in each way so you are authentically getting the information in a way that is in alignment with your delivery.

Psychic work, also called intuitive guidance, is when you are reading another person's energy. The information comes from your higher self, and as you look into their energy, you are able to see what may be happening to them. Depending on what type of information you are reaching for, it may vary in a few different ways.

Aura Reading: This is when you, as a medium, extend your energy into the person's auric field and read through feelings, inner vision and thoughts about what they are currently believing. Your thoughts, choices and beliefs create your reality. Your aura is a living energy and vortex around you that shows you the potential of where you are heading in life based upon what you are vibrating.

For example, say a woman comes to me and wants to find her soulmate, yet when I tune into her, I see she doesn't trust men, she believes all the good ones are taken, or there is no one out there for her. It will be hard for me to find a man in her future that will be there. Sometimes, I see this as a potential partner really far away. I may see that she needs to upgrade her thoughts, beliefs and abilities to put herself out there before that will manifest.

Suppose I meet a man who tells me he is working towards a new career. In that case, I look into his aura and see that he's been studying, applying himself, meeting people within the field, dressing the part, acting the part, and completely changing himself to become that reality. I will most likely tell him that the job is right there, he is so close, and this is coming into fruition.

Your future is very much based on what you put into it today. So, if you are looking for a new life or a changed outcome, you will need to apply yourself and bring it to life in order for it to manifest.

Now, when doing aura readings, you are reading potential. This means that sometimes a medium may see something for you, yet it never manifests. This means it's living in your aura but won't come to fruition unless you move your energy towards it. This is why some predictions do not come true, and others do. If a medium says it's right there, I see this happening, or it's coming into play now. You have aligned your thoughts, beliefs and actions to become this reality.

Soul Reading: A medium extends its energy on a soul level, reading soul to soul. When you read a soul, you read into what it longs for, strives for and wants to create in this lifetime. A soul reader will be able to go beyond the thinking mind of what should be or how to do it and will go into the deeper need and calling of the person receiving this reading. Soul readings are a beautiful way to look at purpose and meaning in life and go beyond the thinking mind. You have a unique soul and blueprint for life with many potentials and feelings. When you lean into your soul, it shares what it truly wants out of this lifetime.

Evidential Mediumship: This is a different way to connect. It's by the medium extending their energy and reaching out to touch the spirit world. They do this by thought, intention and raising their vibrational energy to love. The energy comes from behind and around the medium. The medium uses their sensitivity to receive information through feeling, inner vision, knowing, hearing and taste/smell. The medium shares the information with the client, which the client validates through a *yes or no,* and '*I am not sure',* from the information. The medium stays with the spirit to share the information given, providing evidence of the afterlife, who it is that is there, as well as a message for the client. These readings are not predictive, they are evidential. They bring people healing, comfort, and proof that their loved one is with them.

Psychic Mediumship: When a medium extends their energy to the client, reading them psychically and expands their energy out to connect with a loved one in spirit. They are disciplined to know where the information is coming from: either spirit or the client's aura. They may start one way and then shift another way. Being able to listen deeply to the spirit world and its evidence, as well as being connected to the client's energy, is all at the same time. In development classes, I teach this by having my students place their right hand up when connected to a loved one in spirit, then flip to psychic and lift their left hand. I have them alternate so they know where the information is coming from. This is practice, discipline and focus. This is the most popular reading style in Canada and can be very powerful when done correctly. It needs to come from an authentic space where the medium knows who they are getting the information from and how.

Guide Readings: This is done by doing psychic and mediumship work at the same time, but instead of the loved ones in spirit coming from behind or around the medium, it works through their sensitivity differently. As the medium, you will see guides standing alongside the client. I find their frequency quite different than loved ones in spirit. With departed loved ones, there is a density. Their energy comes through your nervous system being able to share the information that they want to communicate. Reading guides are a very high light frequency, which you can train yourself to see standing around them. I understand that how a person receives information is different for each medium, but for me, when I look at a client and intentionally open myself up to see guides, I see them standing around them. Sometimes, as I am sharing information with them about what is happening in their life, I may see a specific guide stand alongside them that shows them they are helping. For example, this may be a healing guide while dealing with a health problem or a music guide when they are opening themselves up to song writing. When someone is changing careers or really building themselves up in their careers, I may see a guide standing with them to help assist in this new endeavour.

You are never alone walking this path in life. Your guides come as helpers and assisters to guide you in your lives and the changes that you make. Writing this book, I became very aware of new presences standing around me, assisting me in writing.

Guides don't always appear as people. Guides come in ways you feel comfortable seeing them. For some, it's angels, animals, colour frequency, and for others, it's just energy and light. However you receive them, they're completely unique to you, and take on form for you. They are just frequencies of energy and light.

Psychic & Mediumship Exercise

Psychic Exercise:

Sit down in a chair and have someone sit across from you face to face. I usually like to allow a bit of space so you are not touching knee to knee.

Sit upright, feet on the floor and have your partner do the same. Take a minute to clear your head and close your eyes, focusing inward. This helps you move your awareness from your mind and relax into your natural intuitive state.

Become aware of yourself and how you feel. Make sure you are in a good headspace and feeling clear when you practice this. Do your Sitting in The Power exercise first to get comfortable shifting your intention to energy awareness.

With your eyes closed, practice extending your energy forward to touch your partner's spirit. Simply do this by intention and draw your energy towards them. Allow yourself to connect to them. You can practice this like a ping-pong ball. Expanding your energy out, touching their spirit, and then letting it come back and forth until you feel you have made a connection.

You can also practice giving them a warm, energetic hug. This is a way to know you are connecting to your partner and not someone else. Picture it like a bubble, and you are wrapping them into it, kind of like an energy vortex. Keep this connection as you allow yourself to notice the subtle shifts that begin to happen while you are in their energy field.

Allow room for images flashing to you, shifts in energy as you enter their field, and what you have noticed since moving into their space. Pay attention to how you receive information, as it may be visually, through feeling, or even hearing. Let yourself immerse in their energy until you are ready to start to speak.

Share with them what you are getting. Share with your partner what you feel, what images come to you as you receive them and what you feel drawn to tell them. Allow yourself to unfold in what you are saying, picking up and experiencing.

You will know it's theirs if you are aware of your own energy first. When you enter their field of energy, all of a sudden, a shift will happen that was not there before you did this. Trust what comes and be brave enough to share it with your partner. This is how you start developing the language of communication. Let psychic information just come. You will start to develop a language the more you do this, as what you receive will be relevant in a way you can understand and communicate it.

When you are finished, pull your energy back and disconnect. This is very important to do and is required in disciplining yourself. Once you are finished, step away, let go and end the energetic connection. Once you feel yourself again, you are back. It is very important you do this so you don't pick up on everybody all the time. This can lead to burnout and not knowing where you start, and another one begins. You are responsible for your own energy.

Evidential Mediumship Exercise:

Sit down in a chair and have someone sit across from you face to face. I usually like to allow a bit of space so you are not touching knee to knee.

Sit upright, feet on the floor and have your partner do the same. Take a minute to clear your head and close your eyes, focusing on the light within you.

Become aware of your inner light and coming from a place of pure love. Make sure you are in a good headspace and feeling clear when you practice this. Do your Sitting In The Power exercise first to get comfortable shifting your awareness.

With intention, state that you are practising evidential mediumship and you are connecting with a loved one in spirit for your partner. Expand your energy outward and allow yourself to connect to the light around you to connect with a loved one in spirit. Then, using your sensitivity, let the subtle energy of a spirit come to you. Patiently allow room and stay open until you feel you have made a connection.

It may feel like a warm, energetic hug. A feeling or breeze on one side of your body. Tingles on your neck or a presence standing with you. This is a way to know you are connecting to a loved one in spirit and not some random energy. In mediumship, spirit comes to you. As you practice opening up and expanding your awareness, they will make their presence known. Keep this connection as you allow yourself to notice the subtle shifts that begin to happen while you are in their awareness.

While connected to spirit, allow room for images to flash to you, or subtle awareness of feelings, or words. All this may happen since setting the intention to connect. Pay attention to how you receive information, as it may be visual, feeling-based, or hearing. It also could be all of those. Let yourself blend with spirit's energy until you are ready to share with your partner what you are receiving.

Share with them what you are getting in the most natural way you are receiving it. Share with your partner what you feel, what images come to you and what you feel called to tell them. Allow yourself to let the communication unfold. It will unravel as you are connected to spirit and sharing what you are picking up on to your partner.

An example of this would be:

I have a man, a woman, etc. He is showing me a farm and has tools with him, etc.

Or I have a woman here, and she is showing me her passing in a hospital bed.

Or I have a young man here, and he's riding his bike down a mountain.

Each loved one in spirit comes through uniquely. As you reach out to connect, let them fill in the details of what they bring you. Don't go looking; you'll get back into your head again. Let the space fill within. Let your energy tell you a story. If you hear sound, share what you are hearing. Stay calm, connected and in the flow.

Mediumship is done in the moment, not in hindsight. This means the mediumship is alive at this moment; you do not resort back to memory. You stay with the spirit communicator in the now and stay present to what they are bringing you. Let this be an opportunity to learn the language of what they are showing you.

If you try this and nothing happens, go back to Sitting in the Power. Practice this often until you feel a connection to spirit. Do not rush or force it, it will come to you when you are ready.

The Clairs

Each person has natural gifts and intuitive abilities waiting to unfold. We all have a dominant ability that may stand out more than the others, but your abilities will naturally open through development. It's kind of like the petals of a flower opening one by one. Your psychic development can very much look like that too.

In the movie *Twilight,* each character has a unique gift. Edward Cullen had the gift of telepathy (inner hearing), Alice had the gift of premonition (seeing the future) and Jasper could feel other people's feelings (an empath). It's important to remember that each person has their own expression of the divine working through you. These are natural gifts you come in with, and sometimes you don't notice until they are pointed out by another, or you look into them to see which one is expressing through you.

Below is a guide to the clairs, which are different ways of receiving psychic information. Some of which you may be dominant in, and others you could strengthen that are maybe just starting to show. Putting your intention and awareness on them is like giving the flower the water it needs.

Clairsentience is when you use your sense of feeling to interpret messages. Empaths are clairsentient as they feel what others are feeling, and when unaware, they take it on without knowing. Training as a medium, you have to identify what is yours and what is the other person's. You have to use discernment, and train yourself to feel things as messages and guidance.

All evidential mediums use their ability to feel first. In mediumship, you use your nervous system to connect with a departed loved one. Through the connection of sentience, the medium blends their energy with the spirit and is able to interpret what they are receiving. For example, *"I have a father here, and he shows me he had anger issues."* The medium will feel the feeling of anger run through their system.

Another example is, *"I have a really depressed young man here who tells me he died from suicide."* The medium will feel a feeling of depression or despair run through them.

In teaching mediumship, the most common obstacle mediums face is the inability to feel or feeling too much, both of which block the flow of information. If you are talking too fast you won't have enough pausing to be able to feel what's coming through. Mediumship will show you where you are blocking yourself, bringing things to the light. As you learn to feel them deeper or go there, it will not only help you and free you up but also open up your mediumship.

Clairsentience, to me, is the most important faculty of mediumship to spend time developing, and you cannot control or rush it. Often, clairsentience is underdeveloped because it seems cooler to see or hear Spirit, so people spend more time trying to activate those abilities. But sentience is the base of all your work. It will allow you to feel the essence of the communicator, help you interpret what they are really trying to say and why they came, and feel the emotions so that healing can occur between the spirit and the sitter.

Energy work, body work, breathwork, meditation and counselling are great ways to access emotions locked within the body.

Clairvoyance: This ability is about using your third eye, the sense of inner seeing, to see. It can be subjective and objective, meaning subjective clairvoyance is when you see from within.

For example, close your eyes and picture a red house. Did you see it? If so, this is using your subjective clairvoyance for inner vision. When you use your clairvoyant abilities, it is to imagine, create, and envision the world within your mind's eye.

Objective clairvoyance is when you see spirit physically. This type of clairvoyance is much rarer. Most mediums I know work mainly subjectively if that makes you feel better.

I have seen objectively a handful of times, which shocked me each time.

When I teach clairvoyance to my students, they often tell me they don't have clairvoyant abilities, but when I explain it by seeing it within their minds' eyes, they are surprised to learn this is what it is. They assume when someone says, "*I am seeing a man standing here",* that they literally mean they see a spirit physically standing in front of someone. But they don't actually see them there directly, they see it clairvoyantly. The vision appears on the screen within their mind.

I was always a very imaginative child, so my subjective clairvoyance was always open. But it was when I became an acrylic painting artist at 30 that my clairvoyance started to open up in sharp detail. Using colours, imagery, and shapes and imagining something in life, my abilities sharpened. My inner world became a part of my life instead of relying on my physical eyes to get me there. When practising clairvoyance, I recommend doing guided meditations where you are being guided to envision, to take inner journeys and picture things with your mind's eye. I also recommend art, photography, and the creation of projects. With these, you need to envision first before you can create it. Clairvoyance is excellent for goal setting, intending and creating your reality. It allows you to create the world you live in and trust yourself more.

Using your clairvoyant abilities, you envision how your brain can best interpret images. You are taking images from your past and surroundings. When mediums do mediumship, they often get flash images or see things from their own past to make sense of what they are seeing. It's working through your mind and your memory. This is important to know when developing clairvoyance. That what you see within your mind's eye is subject to interpretation. Sharing what you see involves understanding the imagery. This can greatly heighten interpretation when you incorporate clairsentience with your clairvoyance. Then, you see and feel together, giving you a deeper understanding of what you are getting.

Clairaudience: This ability is to be able to hear spirit. This is also a subjective and objective clair, allowing you to hear spirit outside you like a voice and from within. It is rare to "hear" outside of you, and this may come in times of danger when you are being guided back to safety or randomly hearing sound or a voice in mediumship development. The strongest clairaudients I know are musicians. They have the gift of hearing sound, tone and vibration through frequency. When I practice clairaudient exercises with my students, we usually practice picking up an imaginary phone and listening for a reply from spirit. We listen for familiar sounds, voices and tones to be able to interpret what is being heard.

For myself, this was the last clair for me to develop. I was strongly clairsentient, clairvoyant and claircognizant. But a couple of years into my development, I started feeling the urge to play the piano again as I had done as a child. As I retaught myself to read music and play, I noticed that my clairaudient abilities resurfaced. I remember that I had this firmly in my younger years and teen years as I took music lessons and was in our high school band. But I tuned it out. As I retaught myself music, my hearing increased quite quickly, leading me to hear spirit more in sound communication.

One of my students said to me once, *"Nicole, why do you want to teach us how to hear voices? Isn't that insanity?"* I shared that there is a big difference between hearing voices and hearing 'voices'. Tuning into our intuition and listening can be our greatest asset in life. It can be a lifesaving tool and a way to stay connected to yourself. Your intuition is you, only wiser, so you want to learn to hear. But I cannot train you to hear voices that are harmful or unsafe unless you are unstable in your mental health, taking substance use and/or on a bad path for yourself. Those voices are different and may lead you to harm.

How do we know the difference? The voice of spirit is kind, loving, encouraging, empowering, and has your best interests. The voices outside of yourself you could hear if you are unwell would be harmful, dangerous, grandiose, unhealthy and possibly lead to death, suicide or hurting another human. Know that if you are hearing those types of voices, seek medical attention immediately, as it can cause damage and harm to your life and potentially those around you.

If you want to develop your clairaudience, I'd recommend listening to classical music, playing music, listening to audiobooks, and increasing your listening skills instead of talking. Take the time to listen to nature and the sounds around you. Begin to heighten your awareness just by intention.

Recently, I attended a silent retreat. Sitting in silence for five days dramatically heightened my clairaudient skills to a new level. By taking away my voice and being guided to envision and sit in silence, it felt like my hearing was heightened because I allowed room for it, and everything else wasn't necessary.

Claircognizant (clear knowing): The best way to describe this clair is that you know, but you don't know how you know, as you know. Sometimes, I call this wisdom, but it also goes beyond that, as it does not require feeling, seeing, hearing or anything else, it's just knowing deep within you. Of all the clair's, this one is the hardest to misinterpret, as it comes from within, so when you get it, you know.

I find this clair is born within you. It comes with you from your eternal soul. It also can grow throughout this lifetime as you deepen your life experience and wisdom. It just knows…

Practice following through on knowings to develop this deeper. Every time one comes in (like *I should do this*), just do it and say thank you. The more you follow through and appreciate, the stronger these knowings will affect your life.

My fellow medium friends and I talk about how the longer we have been practising mediumship, the stronger our knowings gets in mediumship. This is because, as you attune your energy and vibration to spirit, spirit doesn't have to work as hard to get your attention and get its point across. It comes as knowing. It comes quickly from within, and they may use your familiarity with the language of spirit to communicate with you.

Clairaugustance/Clairolfactance: This is the ability to taste and smell psychically. Have you ever entered a room and suddenly smelt a cigarette, only to discover no one smoked? Or smelt your grandmother's perfume behind you while getting ready for work? This is all psychic smelling. Sometimes, it can be so strong you are unsure if it's literal or if you are smelling from within. Again, this can be subjective and objective. Spirit has a way of creating smell from nothing. If I were to tell you to imagine smelling and tasting orange and you do that, this is using your clairaugustance.

Taste and smell can open up spontaneously without effort or trying. I also find that some loved ones in spirit love to use scent to bring their presence into knowing. When I started offering mediumship sessions, I remember this young lady in her 20s coming to see me. I was taken back by the smell of old ladies' perfume on her, telling myself not to make it a big deal because I needed to read her and not talk about why she smelt like The Bay's perfume department (a department store in Canada). The smell was so overbearing that I held my breath for a moment, wondering if the smell would give me a migraine later. During the session, I brought through this lady's mother, giving her evidence and reconnection that she needed. When the lady got up to leave the session, she asked me if she could hug me. I said yes, and as I leaned into her, the smell of the old lady's perfume was gone. I was so surprised that the scent of her perfume wasn't sticking to me (because it was so overbearing) that I literally said, *"Oh, I thought you were wearing perfume."*

The lady took a step back and said, *"Never!"* She then explained that she never wears perfume because it's so strong. I told her that when she came in, a strong scent of perfume wafted in with her, and I was surprised she didn't smell it when I leaned in to hug her. She then shared with me that she was not wearing perfume but that her mother, when alive, owned a perfume shop. She never did smell like an old lady with perfume, that was simply her mother bringing her perfume store to me. She said it was such a big part of her life that she was surprised her mom didn't mention it, as she still had her perfume bottles. After that day, I learned what clairaugustance really was and never second-guessed it again.

If you want to practice psychic smelling, I recommend paying attention to scent. When going for a walk, stop and smell the roses, the scent of the trees, pine needles and even the scent of dirt. When walking into a garage, take in the smell or scents you notice in that environment and store these smells in your memory. As you become more aware of the scent around you, you will become fine-tuned for psychic smelling. Now that it's in your memory bank, Spirit can access it for future events. Ask your spirit team to communicate with you in this way, just for fun. To help you practice and develop it.

As you can see, each clair has their own way of communication through spirit. Over time, each clair will develop and open, and you will be able to use all your senses at the same time. You will no longer just see or just feel- you will see, feel, hear, taste, and smell all at the same time. It all becomes one and is a part of the communication. Be patient with yourself as each clair develops and unfolds. There is no rush, as Spirit will gift them to you in your unfoldment when you least expect it. Once they are opened, they will always be there for you to access again. Part of developing your clairs is about coming back into your body and using your senses for a whole new purpose.

Playing Your Cards Right

"Do the best you can until you know better. Then when you know better, do better." - Maya Angelou

One of the main reasons I see people close back down in their development of mediumship is because they saw an unpleasant premonition and didn't know what to do with it. I have heard of people having a dream of a loved one dying in a car crash, only to have them pass from a car accident a few days later, or having a vision of a family member having a miscarriage, only for them to have a miscarriage a month later. These situations cause people to close down their sensitivity and not want to see things. What they don't always understand, though, is that you can ask spirit not to show you these things.

You are the one who is in control- meaning you get to decide what it is you know, see and open yourself up to. If you don't want to use your psychic powers to predict death, don't! I sure don't. I even have it on my website next to the booking link: *"I do not predict death."* This gives me peace, knowing I will not be pressured in these situations. I don't want to know most of the time, which means spirit won't show me. This also goes with situations where things are not always helpful for you to know. When building your relationship with spirit, you use your intention to open up gracefully in a way that makes you feel safe. I had a student who told me that she wanted to develop, but what was stopping her was that she didn't want to cause anyone harm. I reminded her that was a beautiful intention and that, as she developed, she included that in her intentional prayers. She wanted to uplift people and cause no harm, helping them feel uplifted and empowered in their experience, not leaving them worse.

Remember, you have much more control than you give yourself credit for. When it comes to your intuitive and mediumistic abilities, you get to direct what you let in and what you don't. We are sensitive beings, and yes, we automatically shut down when we don't want to know something. It's easier than you think it is to block information. Haven't you ever been in love with the wrong person, only to convince yourself that those red flags you're feeling are not accurate? Give yourself a break. We are human, and sometimes, we need to go through a situation, even if it will throw us into an emotional whirlwind.

When you are opening up your abilities, stay open to the gifts that are trying to prosper- be it spiritual healing, evidential mediumship, or intuitive guidance. But also set parameters for yourself of what you are willing and ready to let in. There is no need to scare yourself, and no need to go too dark either!

There will also be times when you know things, and you will have to take accountability for how you say something to someone. Something I have noticed within myself, as well as going to other readers or watching mediums work, is when a message needs to be said, the medium will say it over and over again. This is done in different ways, at other times, and in wording so you can hear them. Pay attention to this. The message is usually very simple. Only the human mind complicates things or needs to take time to let it sink into their consciousness.

There are times I get that clearly a relationship is not going to work, yet I know I am not supposed to say that to someone who is engaged and about to get married. You have to mind your own business. There was also a time when I saw a woman losing her baby before delivery and I was saying almost anything I could to get the subject off of her future and having a child. You will have to learn discernment about what you say and what you see—playing the tape forward and recognising if what you are saying is helpful for their soul's evolution at the moment or harmful. We all know that we still need to live, and we cannot spiritually bypass or skim over aspects of our lives just because we want to. We still need to live our free will lives, and maybe this relationship that I am seeing that's not good for someone is exactly what they need to go through in order for them to claim their power again or see what they need to do with their life.

When I was a young adult, older people in my life would often love to give me unsolicited advice, but I wanted to have my own experience. The older and wiser I get, the deeper my understanding of people, situations and things that someone else may not be able to see. But it does not mean I have to speak up or say anything. I have learned to let people have their own experience.

The way I treat a reading is I let people know that the more specific the question, the more specific an answer. I give them guidance, but they may still need to go through an experience to gain their own wisdom. Sometimes, I do need to wake people up. For example, how many times are you going to give this person a chance? They have already shown you who they are and they're not changing!

As you give readings and practice, you will learn to gauge what is appropriate to say and what isn't. Remember that sometimes a person asks a question hoping you will give them the answer they want to hear, but you will know that's not the outcome. You will find ways to deliver messages in ways they can hear you without sugarcoating it. For example, I see an even better man in your future!

You will not be perfect every time. Sometimes, things slip out, and you wish they hadn't. But you are human, and owning your mistakes is okay, as it strengthens your craft in the future. The longer you do this work, the better you will know what's okay and not okay to say to someone.

Just remember this rule of thumb: be a person of increase. Leave people better than you found them. Inspire and empower them. People come to readings because they want to feel better- know that you can do that with truth. The power of love you are connecting with to bring the information through is always loving and kind. And there is always good news to share!

Chapter 6: The Practice

~

Working As A Medium

From the day I opened my doors in private practice, July 1st, 2012, to the beginning of February 2015, I worked part-time giving healings and tarot readings. My clairvoyance was getting stronger, and my business was getting busier, so much so that I took the risk of leaving my day job to carry out this work full-time.

I was working four days a week in an addiction residential treatment centre on Vancouver Island, BC, as a support worker. I enjoyed the work at first, but over the year and eight months I worked there, my heart could no longer take all the sorrow, deaths and vicarious trauma of working with people with addiction. It was just too big for me, and I found over time of getting to know some of the patients, seeing them come through the centre once, twice or even with some three times, that it was really sad to hear of a sudden passing, after they left the centre from an overdose. Even in treatment, they could not be cured of their illness but had to make the choice to dramatically change their lives if they wanted to recover.

A couple of weeks after I left that job, I was in the bakery down the street from my house. I was buying a muffin from the local bakery and coffee shop, which was quite a social place to hang out and meet people.

Behind me, at the corner of my eye, I saw one of the long-term patients I knew when I was at my job, standing behind me called Brad. I went to pay for my food, hoping that when I turned around, I could take a better look, as he looked so well. As I turned around, though, he wasn't standing there. Confused, I looked around the corner, into the coffee shop and outside. He was nowhere to be seen.

Weird, I thought to myself as I made my way to walk back to my house. As I was walking up the hill towards my house, I got this gust of wind feeling ride up my back, then I felt Brad standing next to me. I could sense him standing there, but he wasn't actually there physically.

I was aware of my clairvoyant abilities getting stronger. More and more spontaneous mediumship (connecting with loved ones in spirit) started happening to me.

"Oh my god", I thought, *"he's gone"*.

Brad stood next to me in spirit. He was being his usual upbeat self, being everywhere at once. He had high energy, and was cheeky, but he wasn't there. I went into the house, and he followed me. I went upstairs to my healing room, and he followed me. At this point in my development of mediumship, I wasn't totally clear on how to turn this off yet, as it was so loud.

"Hi Brad, I see that you are dead. But what do you want me to do?"

"Talk to those left behind." He quickly answered back.

I shook my head. *"Nope. That's not how this works, Brad. I am not like American TV star Teressa Caputo; I cannot walk around giving everyone messages, I do not have my own TV show, and I am not going to be the town's crazy person. If you want me to talk to those left behind, your friends, family, you will have to have them contact me."* And I left it at that.

Brad left, and he vanished out of my sight and room. I was clear on one thing: if I was going to be a messenger for spirit, I would not go out of my way to pass messages. The phrase "don't shoot the messenger" rang in my head. I wasn't that kind of person, and I didn't believe I had to be.

Ten days later, I got an email from a lady asking me for a mediumship reading. She said she knew I didn't advertise for giving mediumship and was more a tarot reader, but that she knew a friend of a friend who knew me and knew that I worked at the addiction treatment centre. She also said that I may know who she is trying to contact in spirit, as she was aware I worked where he went for treatment and that maybe it would help that I understood his background.

My eyes widened as I looked at the email. Holy smokes, I thought, he actually achieved it. I wrote her back immediately. How soon can you come? I hoped she would take me up on an immediate offer.

When she came, I shared with her what had happened to me. I was waiting for someone he knew to contact me. She was touched and glad to hear he had gone out of his way to get us in touch. I was thrilled I could help, and it was easy to connect with him and pass on whatever he had to say.

After she left the reading, she was teary-eyed. She knew that she had her whole life ahead of her and that Brad would not be the last love of her life. As she left, she asked if we could do this again in the future. I said I would love to be there for her in any way I could.

I sat in my room after she left. The tears fell down my face as I reflected on what had just happened. It saddened me to see this beautiful young woman lose the man of her dreams to addiction. He really did love her, but his addiction overpowered him. I felt anger, thinking about how much I hated that job because of all the people who died of addiction and how well they were when they were in full treatment— seeing and hearing that they couldn't make it on their own felt so unjust. I questioned why I ever worked there and put myself through that for a 16-dollar-an-hour job. I had never done work that was as heartbreaking, stressful, and gut-wrenching as I did for this job. I shook my head a little, hoping I would never have to return to a job while doing the work I felt was my calling, which was working for spirit.

Then Brad spoke to me… *"What if that job was there to get you ready for what is to come in your future? What if your time working there was to prepare you for all the people you will help moving forward who lost their loved ones to addiction?"*

At that moment, it all flashed before me. The knowledge and understanding I had gained about this vicious disease. All that I had to grow from, learn and work with while working in addiction.

He was right, I thought.

From that moment forward, I have never stopped working with mothers, fathers, sisters, brothers, husbands, wives, siblings, and friends who have lost their loved ones to addiction. I have done it so often that I started to wonder if certain spirits were handing out my business card on the other side.

I'll rarely give a reading to a client where I don't have some connection or understanding with the loved one in spirit that comes through. Your loved ones in spirit look to see who is open (mediumistic) and how they can connect themselves with their person in physical form and get the medium to pass the message. The way they showed me it was like looking down from an eagle's view and seeing who is lit up like a lighthouse and close enough by. When they find the lighthouse (the open and available medium), they start working their magic to guide them to you. When people ask why so and so didn't come through, I mention it's not that they aren't there; they didn't step forward. Sometimes, there is a need for someone else instead of who they hoped for. But there is no mistake, and you will notice if you check out a few different mediums that every single one will bring your loved one in spirit differently than the others. This is because of how mediums filter information through their brains and comprehend information, just like how, if you got 20 people to paint the same picture, it would look different for each person. This is because of our perceived lens and what stands out to us. It is easy for certain information to come through and harder for other information. That hard information for you may be super easy for another medium to get.

I also tell people to look around. What platform would your loved ones in spirit want to come through? Were they a public person? Would they like to be brought through in a public demonstration? Or with a celebrity medium like John Edward or James Van Praagh at a live show or broadcasted on TV? Or were they private? Would they prefer the one-to-one intimate time so they can go into deep conversation and detail? Recognising who they were in life can give clues to how and even where they will show up in spirit.

Handing It Back To Spirit

"We cannot do great things. Only small things with great love"- Mother Teresa

Trust that the intelligence that brought you into this world is the same intelligence that will bring you home. If someone you know has passed away and you feel their presence around you right away, it means they are still close to the Earth plane. This can be for various reasons. Perhaps they left unexpectedly and feel they need to comfort those left behind. There could be things that have been left unsaid or done. They may try to help bring closure to the family or those left behind, allowing the family to find them or letting them know they are gone. Or they are helping with closing up their life. I feel this often when I am involved in celebrations of life directly after their passing. Heck, I even feel like they sit with me when I write their eulogy, ensuring I don't 'miss anything.

Know that your loved one in spirit doesn't actually need your help to cross them over. But know that your prayers, intentions and good thoughts always help. If you feel like a loved one is hanging around you right after they died and you feel they are staying a little longer than comfortable, here is something you can do.

1.   Light a white candle (to represent the light and their transition)

2.   Say an intentional prayer: *"Great Spirit, please take it from here. Please support (loved one's name here) in their transition. I call in all the helpers, guides, and beings of the greatest good to take his hand and guide him/her/them from here."*

3. Do what I did with Brad and tell them that if they want you to talk to their loved one in spirit, to bring them to you. Then let go and know it's in their hands.

4. Sit and bask in the light. Feel the room fill with love as you hand it over to Spirit. It was never your job to carry them anyway.

Always keep it simple. Ground yourself, set the intention and put the focus on love and give it back to Spirit. They know what they are doing. Remember, they sent you here! They know how to get you home too.

Another thing to remember: when you are not tuned into mediumship fully, giving your loving intention and power into the spirit world, you can get half the information. This means that you are tuned into multiple radio channels at once. Remember, as I mentioned earlier, spirit communicates in the vibration of love. When you are half-focused and thinking of something else, you can easily misinterpret what is being said. A lot of time, they are just there. Keep it simple, and use prayer to guide you.

July 2023

One of my students, Michelle, emailed me first thing in the morning. *"Nicole, my cousin just died last week, and we are heading to his funeral in a couple of days. He wasn't a believer, but he is hanging around. He seems distressed and I feel he is asking for my help. Can you help me with this? I'm not sure what to do."*

I was invited to an outdoor summer party in the Cowichan Valley that evening and Michelle would be there. We decided we'd meet up at the party and take a curious look at what was going on.

When I arrived at the party, Michelle found me immediately. Synchronistically, she was walking right towards me when I was walking in. We disappeared behind the house and found a place on the grass to sit together undisturbed.

I shared with her a bit about my understanding of loved ones in spirit hanging around. We imagined lighting a candle in the grass (to represent the light) and sat together face to face. Before I even had a moment to talk, I could feel her cousin, who had recently passed, staring right at us. It was like the intense stare a dog gives you when you are eating food in front of them, and they want it.

We closed our eyes and moved our awareness into our hearts as we started to build the power together. When I felt the energy shift, I opened with an intentional prayer, *"Great Spirit, we welcome your presence to fill this space. We recognise the same intelligence that brought Michelle's cousin to this world will be the same intelligence that will bring him home. We call in all the support needed from the unseen world. All the guides, guardians, loved ones in spirit, whoever may take over from here with his transition. We hand this over to you."*

Just as I spoke those words, we both felt the wind pick up and start gusting by. Tingles moved up and down our spines, and our arms were covered in goosebumps. We smiled as we felt the presence of Spirit all around us, her cousin in spirit and this huge weight off Michelle's chest. It was like whatever pressure she felt she needed to carry was lifted. I felt this sudden feeling of grace, taking all that no longer needed to be handled.

Michelle spoke a few words to her cousin as we basked in the glory of infinite love all around him. The sense of peace was immense.

We closed with a thank you and continued with our evening. The work was done and we gave the responsibility back to Spirit and let them do their job by taking it from there.

When I hear about mediums feeling spirits following them around, they often feel like they are supposed to be doing something. Now they are in spirit, they are aware of your light, that you have the ability to see them. So, they may hang around you because you are open, kind of like a lighthouse. Feel free to take the pressure off yourself and hand it back to Spirit at any time or moment. Just like your job in life is not to take too much on, in spirit it's the same.

181

Mary - June 2004. Picture taken at my hairdressing
graduation day June 2004.

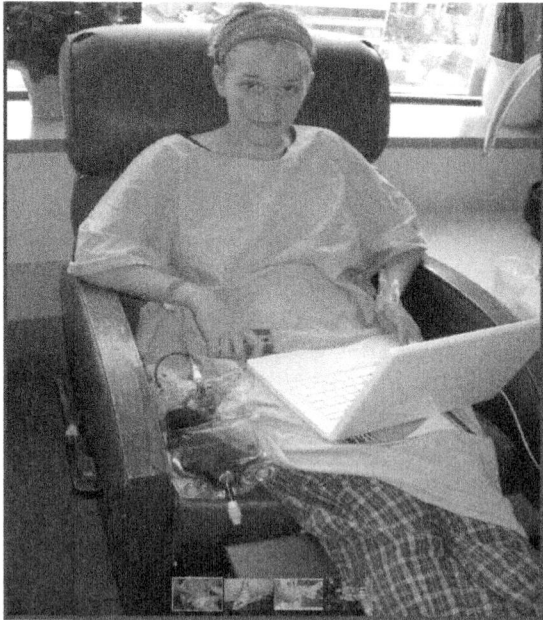

My week-long stay at the hospital in Vancouver, BC, after my
visitation from Spirit. July, 2007

Graduation Day with Dad - Integrative Energy Healing
Certification Program at Langara College Vancouver
BC. - June 2012

I was so excited to launch my first business and work as an
Integrative Energy Healer. - In my home office – 2014

Three generations. My grandmother, mother and I. – 2008

My first trip to Arthur Findlay College in Essex, England -
September 2015

A gift from my grandmother in spirit at the Arthur Findlay
College in 2015

Mediumship Message Night With Jason Goldsworthy. We used
to do a bunch of these when Jason would visit from Germany. -
Victoria BC 2019

Ordination Day to become a Spiritualist Minister with Reverend
Dianne Burrough - May 2021

Ordination Day. With my husband Matthew Ashdown - May
2021

Circle Night at my house with the ladies. We have cakes every week in August because so many of us are Leo's. - August 2023

Our epic Christmas service at Two Worlds with our amazing team! Chairing Heather Thornton, and mediums Lee Shanks, Lana Ryan and I. The mediums are also board members of our centre. - December 2023.

Overdose

When a loved one in spirit passes due to an overdose, there are usually a lot of questions from those left behind to find out if their loved one is okay and what happened. Where I live in the world, there is a fentanyl crisis. Drugs have been laced with fentanyl, so those who may have had inconsistent or low drug use are still dying of overdoses, a population of people who may not have died if this wasn't going on.

Yes, of course, drug use is still a common way to pass away, but being a medium, I have to be discerning to listen deeply to the loved one in spirit while they tell their story. It is not always the story of a drug user who couldn't get their addiction under control. It can be the young 20-year-old with plenty of ambition who didn't use substances, who went to a party and used it for the first time only to die suddenly of a drug overdose because it was laced with fentanyl.

Being a medium, I have worked with many parents, giving messages to their children about their passing and what happened. Parents want to know that their children are okay and are in a safe place despite what has happened to them.

When I have communicated with loved ones in spirit who have gone through addiction, they have shared what it was like for them. For heavy drug users who couldn't get clean, I found a theme that when it came to their death: they weren't really living and came to a place where they just didn't always care if they lived or died. They had lost all hope for life, and not waking up the next day wasn't necessarily bad. They were done fighting, and this was a way out. I always feel such self-responsibility from the loved ones in spirit about their passing. They are very rarely a victim when they talk about their death and their addiction from the spirit world. They can see that their life led to certain circumstances. Sometimes, it's just harder to hear for those left behind.

When I have communicated with loved ones who have passed on and died suddenly from addiction where their drugs were laced, there is usually a surprise factor to their death. They didn't see it coming. They say they fell asleep, felt heavy, and didn't wake up in the physical world but in the spirit world. A common theme is that they feel at peace with their passing, with acceptance that it was their time to pass on. Most often, we have no idea why we lose the ones we love. But I like to believe that when we are on the other side with them, it will make more sense then. We are all one. Who knows what agreements we made with each other before stepping into this lifetime as family and close friends.

I find from communicating with loved ones in spirit who passed from addiction that they are accepting and are okay with being in spirit. Of course, it hurts them to see their loved one on Earth in so much pain and suffering from their loss, but time and time again, they will share that they are okay, that they are resting, and that life continues for them on the other side, not to worry and know that they are looked after. The other important thing is that, even though they may have died from an overdose or laced drug, they will hold the responsibility that they willingly took it.

I had a mom sit with me once, and her daughter had passed to spirit through an overdose that seemed to have been a laced drug. Even though she struggled with addiction, she was sober for quite some time. Her death was sudden, and she was not using or showing signs of using from family and friends that day and weeks prior. It was a slip, but a slip that cost her life. Her mother was distraught, suffering, and unable to cope with what reality had faced her with. Her daughter was a beautiful woman who had helped many people and did not deserve this. The mother wanted to hold accountable those who she believed caused this.

I felt her daughter stand next to me. She placed her hand on my shoulder, and I heard her say, "*Mom, no one shoved the drugs down my throat; I took them willingly. This is my responsibility, even if it's hard to believe.*"

I shared with her mother what I heard, and the tears rolled down her face. It's easier to blame than to accept what is, even when there is so much turmoil and injustice in the world.

A lot of spirits when they show me their death, talk about going to a holding space after they pass away to rest. For many who struggled with addiction, life was exhausting and chaotic, having a resting place is exactly what they needed.

The Holding Space

I was a guest minister at the Cowichan Valley Spiritualist Church Of Healing And Light and was giving a service. Regarding the Evidential Mediumship part, I brought through a lady who let me know she had recently passed. She showed me how colourful in life she was. She was good at everything. She had a beautiful garden, was a wonderful cook, relentlessly helped others, was a huge animal lover, was an uplifter, an Earth angel and wanted to communicate with someone in the room who needed to know she was okay after the recent passing that was quite traumatic to witness her dying in the hospital. A man raised his hand up, and as we continued the message, it turned out she was his wife, and she had just passed away a couple of weeks earlier.

After the service, he shared that he needed that message and thanked me for what came through so clearly from her. He asked if he could come to see me for a private reading and a few weeks later he came so I could explore if there was anything else she needed to say. When I tuned into his wife, she was there, but not as clear as that day she came when I was giving a message at the service. It was like she was wrapped in blankets or wrapped in a warm cocoon filled with love. She was in a resting place.

The man had so many questions. Who had she met up with? Where had she been? What was the other side like? But instead of those answers rushing through, it felt like a pause in the space. There was nothing to say because she was resting where she was. It's like asking someone a question when they are napping - they are there, but not really. They are listening but not doing anything.

It is quite common for people who suffered at the end of their lives to go into this holding or resting space—a place where they can stay as long as they need without having to go any further. The image I receive is like someone being wrapped in a cocoon or sleeping bag while a band of spirits or angels are around them holding space.

There is nothing someone can do in the physical world to rush their experience through this holding space. Nor should they feel they need to or want to. When a loved one dies, sometimes it is just nice to rest pain-free, held by the divine with nowhere to go, nothing to do but be in the presence and holding of the spirit world. When I communicate with loved ones in spirit who have died of addiction, suicide or a painful illness, I find that they usually rest in this place for a while. When I say a while, it can be anywhere from days to weeks, months to even years. There is no time and space in the spirit world. It is not for us to figure out or judge where someone is. Sometimes, spirits come rushing like horses out of the gates, while at other times, it feels like you're grasping at straws. None of it is wrong, but I go where the energy flows as a medium. So, I go to the spirits who are ready and willing. I try to never force communication. It's kind of like having a conversation with a human who doesn't want to talk to you. It goes nowhere, fast.

The man asked if he could come back many months later, when he had processed his grief more and when his wife may be more open to communicating. Another 6-8 months later, he came back.

As I was getting ready for him to come, I could feel the presence of his wife standing on my left side. It was like she was banging pots and pans over my head, letting me know she was there and making it loud enough for me to know she was ready to communicate. It's like the feeling of knowing you have to call someone and, no matter how much you try to do something else, you can't do anything until you address what you feel you have to do first. When the man arrived, my bum barely hit the chair to sit down before I was ready to unleash whatever needed to be said. Sometimes, it feels like I am talking like a chipmunk sped up. I couldn't get through what she had to say fast enough.

He asked me if the reason she had so much to say this time was because she was no longer in the holding space. When I tuned back into his wife, I saw her darting around the room. She was here, there and everywhere. She showed me visions of her expansion and how she could be in multiple places at once. She was giving me multiple pieces of evidence at the same time, and it took me a minute to process it all. It's like looking at a photograph and feeling, seeing, and getting so much from that one picture that it takes a moment to unpack it all and take it in.

"No, she is definitely not still in that holding space," I replied. *"Last time, it felt thick. Today, it feels lighter than air. She is ready, and it seems you are more ready to receive what she has to say. When she came through that time at the service directly after she passed, she wanted you to know she was okay and she made it there. Like a phone call you do when you call home to family to let them know you arrived safely in your travels. There was also her time for herself, her rest. Now that she has gone full circle, she is here and ready to communicate."*

He let this sink in. He was happy to hear his wife was willing to communicate and be present. He needed that, and he learned to be patient. She was adamant that he needed to keep living his life, there was a reason she passed first and needed him to do this part of the journey without her physical presence. He got that. He knew it was part of the deal. That, and she needed him to know she never left him. He smiled, *"My wife was always great at that. She always had a way of making me feel safe. She always promised she'd never leave me. And she never has… even in spirit."*

On Suicide

It was circle night, and I thought I'd try something fun and experiential with my students. They were developing their evidential mediumship, yet they still doubted it was real. I decided to take the names of celebrities who have passed and place them on a piece of paper for an experiment. I folded the pieces of paper with the celebrities' names and handed them out randomly to the group. The intention was that they would hold the piece of paper, without looking at it, and tune in and see if their spirit came to them. I told them not to force or try to figure it out, to close their eyes, allow and wait for a presence to join them. To allow the celebrity to show them how they want to present themselves.

One of the pieces of paper I wrote down was the actor Robin Williams. He had been in spirit for about two years, and his name popped into my head to write on one of the pieces of paper when I was writing them out. I trusted that the celebrity names that came to me were perfect.

This evening was an experiment. Would Robin Williams come to us? If so, how would he present himself?

As we went around the circle, we got to Cait, who was holding the paper with Robin Williams's name on it. She looked at me then around the room, and said, *"Well, when I placed the paper in my hands and closed my eyes, all I saw was an image of a robin bird, but I couldn't get any further than that."*

I smiled and asked her to open the paper. She was shocked when she saw who it was.

"Wow", she exclaimed, her eyes wide with surprise.

Wow, that is right.

Six months passed, and I decided to try this exercise again with another circle group at my house. As I placed celebrities' names on the paper, I heard *"Robin Williams"* pop into my head again. So, I wrote his name, folded it, and placed it in the bowl. As each student reached their hand into the bowl to grab a piece of folded-up paper, I wondered who would get the Robin Williams one. This time, I did the exercise differently - asking them to all join me in a meditation where we'd call in the spirit of the celebrity whose name was on the paper. We all connected, and I walked them through with my voice.

Something magical started to happen. The whole room lit up with light. The sun had begun to shine through the window and brighten the circle room. Birds that weren't there before began singing outside the door. All of a sudden, I noticed I was hit with the giggles. As soon as we finished the meditation, it created a domino effect, and laughter filled the room.

Usually, I can't get one of my students to go first, but this time, everyone wanted to go first. They were all asking if they could go, and one after the other, they shouted, *"I believe I got Robin Williams!"* Then the next person said, *"No, I got Robin Williams!"* And yet another person said, *"No, I got Robin!"*

Half of the room was convinced they had Robin, as the room lit up with this humorous spirit. They felt like someone was playing a trick on them, and they started seeing images within their minds of clowns, movies he had been in and his many funny voices. I don't think we carried on with the exercise after that as we were supposed to, as we were all hit with uncontrollable laughter. One by one, my students started to share what they had got about Robin. Each of us had hairs standing on the back of our necks and chills running through our bodies. Once we tossed the other names aside and accepted that Robin had taken over our circle, we all held hands and joined to him collectively.

We wanted to know if he was okay. Was he judged for his suicide like certain spiritual or religious text would say? Was he all well over there like we imagined?

We got the answer from him in a strong knowing that he was more than okay; he was doing fantastic. He was still a clown, happy with his freedom with where he was and knew his death was a statement about mental health awareness. He was at peace and thrilled to join in spirit with anyone willing to connect. He lightened our spirits that night, and we all felt blissed out by the whole experience. Then again, that's what a mediumship circle is all about.

****

Sudden death by suicide can have many meanings. It is not a one-size-fits-all when interpreting from the loved ones who have crossed this way. They usually have a lot to share about where they are at now, and I find that each spirit has its reasoning behind it and experiences where they are now. Never have I heard about a heart being judged or sent back to Earth. Nor have I ever heard of a soul being trapped between worlds. The spirit world is love. You are here on Earth to have an experience, but there is no punishment for your behaviour when you return home. That is an artificial tail. You will be surrounded by a state of love, like a warm hug from Spirit, knowing you are continuously looked after, regardless of your situation or what has happened to you. There is no forgiveness either because the creator never judged you in the first place. As a medium working with many souls who have chosen to transition this way, I've communicated with many of their thoughts.

Here are some examples of what they have communicated:

- *"I died of mental illness. I was sick, and the voice was so loud I genuinely thought I was doing the right thing."* Usually, a suicide note is present, explaining they cannot do this anymore.

- *"I did it to punish my dad, mom, girlfriend, husband, etc. My death was a statement."* I have seen this in a situation where the son was mad at his father and thought he could get him back by punishing him this way. In this one particular situation, the son did it when he was under the influence of alcohol and was having an intense moment of emotional pain. What felt like a good idea at the time had long-lasting side effects and he came through to apologise for its lasting impact on the dad.

- *"I didn't even know what was going on. My brain was fuzzy, and I wasn't thinking clearly."* They may have been experiencing substance use or on medication that wasn't compatible with the person. I have also seen this with schizophrenia and feeling out of control.

- *"I did it impulsively, and I didn't think it through. I was in a bad mood, and it was a sudden decision."* I have seen this one a lot with men particularly. I was having big feelings, running away and needing space. Death feels like the easy way out.

- *"I couldn't see a future for myself. I felt I was already in enough pain or suffering, and it was my time to go."* This could include those who have mental illness, health issues, old age or fear of growing up and adulting.

- *"I romanticised my death. With organising my affairs, dramatic death notes. I wanted to be a legend. It was like I needed a grand departure."* This one is usually filled with forgiveness and apologies for how their death affected their loved ones left behind. These kinds of people were usually self-obsessed in life and many could not ask for help. One time I brought through a loved one who passed this way, in life he was a service worker. He wanted to make a statement to healthcare providers about how devastating his work was and how he hoped it woke people up to how they treat their staff.

- Very rarely will the spirit communicator regret their decision, and I am not even sure this is possible, stating that this was just how they were meant to go. They are usually shocked at how much it affects and hurts their loved ones left behind. Most likely, it was hard to comprehend because they were in such a unworthy state. Illness of mind can be so debilitating, so horrifically uncomfortable, it can make dying from cancer look like a breeze. The pain is so severe that a shock or a cut would give relief to the mental pain they are in.

However a loved one dies, it is important to know that they are surrounded by love upon their return home. They may stay in the holding space to take a rest for as long as they need, and/or continue to live out their evolution of the soul. Most importantly, they will stay with you for as long as you need. As they cannot die but will be forever in your heart.

Forever In Our Hearts

When my dog Ebony was 18, it came time to put her down. We had been dreading this day since she came into my life. Ebony was the dog I rescued, but she rescued me, when I was 25. She came into my life by chance, and through the following years she helped me graduate from Integrative Energy Healing School at Langara College, move out of the house I previously owned, leave my 10-year career as a hairstylist, leave town and move back to Vancouver Island where I ended up meeting Matthew right away. She was a very special dog. When she came into my life major life shifts happened quickly; she was a dog that helped me through a lot of transition. She was with me when I started my business, and she stayed with us until we bought our home here, and my work was steady. She was old, and I knew it was coming, but saying goodbye to our animals is always way harder than anticipated because of the unconditional love they bring.

We took Ebony to emergency at midnight one night after a whole day of tests at the vet. We weren't sure how soon it was coming, but I knew it would be time once she gave me that look in my eyes. Although I hadn't seen it yet, I trusted when it did happen that I would surrender and take her immediately. That night, around 10 pm, she started struggling with breathing. Usually, for Ebony, I could send her some energy healing, and she would be better 10-15 minutes later, but that night, I heard a strong *"No"* from her, then she looked me in the eyes and said, *"Help."*

We drove an hour to the closest emergency vet hospital that was open, and we called them on the way, letting them know we needed to put her down quickly as she was suffering. I hated that she was suffering and that it had to come to this last moment. I prayed the whole car ride there as Matthew drove. I held her in my arms and held my hand on her heart. I soothed her by telling her we were listening and she wouldn't have to hold on much longer. That this would soon be over, and she would be crossing the rainbow bridge and would have more air to breathe than she'd ever had here. I could feel her little heart beating in my hand, and it was beating fast. I knew how hard it was working. I felt the presence of Spirit around us, and the time passed quickly to get us to the vet hospital.

As we took her in, the vet who was doing the euthanasia was very kind and friendly. She was a young woman in her 30s with a lot of animal experience. She looked at Ebony and told us we were doing the right thing. I kept my hand on Ebony's back of her heart as she lay on the table. I never disconnected from her and talked with her the whole time. The vet gave her an intravenous first to let her sleep so it could be less stressful. I felt her body relax as she fell asleep, and I instantly felt better knowing she was getting out of pain. As she hooked up the intravenous drugs, all of a sudden I saw a visual of her heart being charged with electricity. This visual before my eyes was like energy running around her heart, like the rings of Saturn around the planet. This energy went into my hand, and I felt it run up my left arm, and it started to fuse with my heart. I felt my heart get charged with energy from her heart and witnessed and experienced the whole thing. As Ebony took her last breath in life, her heart fused with my heart. She did not leave. She did not go anywhere; her spirit became a part of my spirit. Her heart was my heart. We were no longer separated through bodies, but we were one.

My heart felt enlarged instantly as I got used to the feeling of her heart being fused with mine. I petted her physical body as she lay there, so peacefully gone, but I no longer felt her spirit with her, her spirit was within me. We drove home in peace that night, knowing that Ebony was no longer suffering, and I placed my hand over my heart for that duration. My heart ached as if I had had a heart attack or had been struck with something unexpectedly charging - like I had been electrocuted. For about three days, my heart ached from the grief but also from the infusion that had happened when she fused her heart with mine.

As I walked down the street the following day, missing her physical presence, I was aware of her presence all around me. It was like a narrator called Ebony lived inside me and could communicate. She assured me we would never be separated again. She was forever in my heart and nothing could separate us, not even life or death. Grieving the physical loss of her presence was a given, but to never see her as gone.

Ebony often visits me in dreams to this day. She always looks like a young puppy, happy to see me and pass along messages. She is always smiling. She was the greatest gift in my life. She helped me through so much, and I am forever grateful to her. But I also know the gift our pets offer us is beyond time and space. They come for a reason- to help us heal and open us up to unconditional love. To be blessed with a pet that is also a kindred spirit is that one gift you never take for granted.

Chapter 7: Compassion

~

Life Ending Before It Began

"When we go someplace, we leave a part of our energy there and we influence more than we can ever imagine." - Dolores Cannon

Trigger Warning: The content below could be upsetting or emotional, as it involves miscarriage, abortion and stillborn babies.

I had a cancellation for a private reading and invited a woman named Lindsay to come for this last-minute session. She said it was very important and asked for an emergency reading. Sometimes I can, and sometimes I can', accommodate such requests, but what I do is hand it to Spirit and, if things align, then it works, but when it doesn't, I have to trust that they get the help they need from the appropriate source, and that is always my prayer. *"Spirit send them the perfect healer, medium, and/or medical professional they need, making it easy for them to find. Thank you"*

When Lindsay came in, she looked as white as a ghost. She looked low to the ground as she walked in, and it felt like her spirit was outside her body. About a year prior, I had seen her once and had vague memories of her, but I did not remember her looking this way the previous time. She seemed different, like something had happened. As I walked her into my office and she sat down, I eagerly looked forward to tuning in to see what was going on for her. When she sat down, she didn't say much. She just waited to see what would happen, her head held low to the ground.

I closed my eyes and said a prayer under my breath that I could help Lindsay and for Spirit to take over to bring through what was needed. As I said this, I noticed this little bright pink light start to travel into the room and merge with me. It was small, luminescent and had the most innocent, childlike energy I had ever witnessed before.

I said to her I felt there was a small child here with me. Lindsay confirmed, yes.

I said to her I felt that this small child that came to me in a pink bubble barely made it to the Earth plane and must have passed before she was even born. Lindsay confirmed this to be accurate as well.

I felt the emotion take over the room as if her spirit had filled every corner of the room and illuminated her light. For an infant that had not even made it Earthside, she was sure communicative, and a part of me was curious how this could even be. How could a baby that wasn't even born make herself so present and communicative when she didn't even have a chance to make it through her birth?

I am always in awe of the intelligence of Spirit, in what they bring, how they come through and what they choose to share and say. This little baby shared with me that she had fulfilled her life purpose despite the circumstances. Her death was no mistake, no fault of the parents or delivery team. She came to Earth to have the experience of being in the womb but had no plan to stay after this.

Lindsay cried as the waves of emotion poured over her. The guilt, the despair of what had happened, and not being able to fully comprehend why this needed to be so abrupt of an ending.

The baby shared some of what it was like for her in the womb, that she chose her parents, she left right on schedule, and there was no reason to feel the guilt and shame her mother had for losing her during childbirth. Despite how hard it was to believe, she was never meant to live a full life.

Lindsay asked what happened - how did she die? What this little child showed me was that she got squished or suffocated in the canal while trying to give birth to her. It was quick, the passage was narrow, and she took the first exit out as she started coming through. I then got an image of Lindsay giving birth and saw all her grandmothers standing over her. They all knew what was happening and were there to comfort her and collect the baby. I saw, even though her soon-to-be daughter died in the canal, that she was surrounded in spirit with support. I saw the image of Lindsay holding her baby with no heartbeat or breath. I saw her cry, as well as the horror and despair falling over her and her partner as they realised there was no happy ending.

Receiving such messages and visions and doing these types of readings are hard. There is no way around it, as I feel everything. It involves going there, being present at the moment and doing my job to be of service to be the medium for both spirit and the client.

This reading stuck with me for days. I even questioned why anyone would put themselves through such a thing, with the possibility of no happy ending with a baby. But really, this instance isn't a common occurrence, and we must be brave to show up for life. Not to mention, having a child isn't always planned, and beautiful children are born every day.

I spoke to another medium about this topic and situation, and she shared that she had lost a baby in her womb as well. I asked her how she dealt with it, thinking to myself that I could not think of anything worse in the world than the loss of a child. *"I know my baby is with me always."* She responded. *"She was with me in my womb, and she is with me from the spirit world. Nothing, I repeat, nothing, can separate us. Even though I do not understand it now, I know that one day, when I am gone, I will be with my baby again, and in the meantime, my loved ones in spirit have her. She is a part of me, growing with me, in my growth and unfoldment of life."* In my opinion, it also made her a stronger medium, more compassionate and caring for others. Actually, I felt she was one of the most compassionate, heartfelt mediums I had ever met.

****

I have heard many stories about the point at which the spirit of the child enters the womb. I have heard that sometimes the spirit waits until the second trimester because there is nothing for them to do, while I have heard other stories that the spirit enters the moment of conception.

What I have noticed in my experience of doing readings is that the spirit of the child shows up many months before the woman is ready to conceive. The spirit child will hang around the mother and father, aligning their energy to begin to prepare for them.

I have given readings and seen a spirit child standing beside them and blended with their loved one and letting them know they could become pregnant very soon. I also know that spirit children wait for their parents to be ready and are not really in a rush either. Sometimes, things have to come into alignment before their entry and they hang around, hoping their influence can get them ready.

I have communicated with unborn children who are only 8-12 weeks pregnant. When I tune in, I am very clear that I have a presence speaking back to me telepathically. Their spirit is there, and they are ready to communicate, even months before arrival, and they hang around in the womb or even around the womb. I have also noticed when I have given readings to pregnant women that they have a bubble of light wrapped around them. It is as if they are being protected from harm. An entourage of spiritual energy is wrapped around them as a barrier to keep their spirit protected from people and harm.

There are also situations where I have communicated with spirit children who were aborted or miscarried early. What I have noticed from aborted children is that they are there usually to wake up their parents. They came for a specific reason, knowing they wouldn't stay for their life, but it was a wake-up call to the mother and father. Some examples of this would be realising they want a child but aren't ready and need to get their life in order. Or that they were using too many harmful substances, leading them to careless situations where they realised there was no going back and ended up pregnant. Or situations where they realised that they were with the wrong partner and needed to not only terminate the pregnancy but end the current relationship.

These are a few examples of things I've witnessed, but if the person is willing, there is always a learning to the situation. The child that came knew this too and offered to be this spirit to help them with their soul's journey.

I had a young man come to see me for a session. His name was Jake, and he was completely distraught from aborting a child with his girlfriend due to their young age and simply not being ready. They were only 20 years old, yet a few years later, this situation still haunted him. He loved his girlfriend, always had, and they were still together. But he had this intrinsic fear that he would experience harsh karma for his actions. He cried out, "*We killed our baby!*" As he said that, this little blue bubble of light flew into the room above his head and said, *"I cannot die."* I shared this with him. They may have terminated the pregnancy due to personal reasons, but you could not kill a spirit. The spirit lives on, this child lives on, and in fact, came in to support him just in that moment when he felt he could not live with himself.

This eased him, knowing I could see his unborn child above him and he could feel the presence just from communicating about it. He was there and still with him despite what had happened. He and I got the same feeling at the same time. When he and his girlfriend were ready and in a good place, this child could may well return to them. I didn't even have to say this to him, we just looked at each other at that moment, and both knew that that was a strong possibility.

Each soul is here for a journey - to learn, grow, and expand. Our loved ones on the other side, whether we know them or not, do use themselves for our soul's development. This includes our unborn children. There are no mistakes in this universe, just learning experiences.

There are many factors that go into miscarriages, and they can greatly vary. Louise L Hay states in her book *"You Can Heal Your Life"* that miscarriages have to do with inappropriate timing. I completely agree that the universe is in perfect order. A lot of times when I meet a woman who has had miscarriages and then had a child again many months later, they can validate that they, too, felt that the child came at the perfect time, and they trusted nature. But there are other times when I feel this analogy doesn't always apply.

Life can very much be a mystery, especially when the child you longed for never came. I can't even count how many near-pregnant women I have met over the years who have come to me for readings. I have seen spirit children around them, and yet they run into miscarriage after miscarriage. Sometimes, the body is just unable to carry a child. Sometimes, they are with the wrong partner; they are more likely going to be happy if they foster or adopt, and sometimes, women realise that they never really wanted a child anyway and are grateful that they didn't have one. But the answers to these questions don't always come in the moment or even in this lifetime. I am a huge fan of hindsight. Instead of trying to get the teaching as quickly as possible to "heal" it and move on, you continue living, let your life play out, and, in time, reflect on your life and see why it never happened the way you imagined it to, as well as what you may have learned from the experience. Sometimes, as humans, we push too hard to make things happen, only to end up with a result that isn't desirable anyhow.

I have had women ask me why I felt that those who didn't really want children or were born in domestic violence or unstable homes are the women who seem to always be getting pregnant. Of course, this is not always the case, but when a stable couple who is married, has a home, good jobs, and a baby room ready but cannot get pregnant, they think of these things.

But the only way I can answer that is because, in those situations, there is a spiritual need. A child can come as a blessing, a wake-up call, an opportunity to break ancestral cycles, and can teach a parent inner child work as well as personal growth and development. Children come when they are called for a soul's evolution. Still, I also feel that in those situations where a stable couple (happily married, happy in their jobs, happy in the home) are unable to get pregnant, their life will take them a different way. And yes, they are worthy of a child and will most likely have one. They will not always get it at the snap of their fingers, but in time and with patience, when a child is ready to show up, they do. And you must stay open to how they arrive as well.

We are all children of God. All of us are special, and none of us are special. We each have come here for a journey different from each other's. Children are one way to help the soul's development, but not the only way. Teachings can come in many forms. For some, it can be the highest learning, while for others, it may come in different forms.

Self-Expression

"Don't die with your music still in you"- Wayne Dyer

I was working with a mother who had lost her 18-year-old son to suicide. Her son came through quickly after several other family members appeared first in her reading. She had waited patiently, hoping he would come, and I noticed that when he stepped forward, she felt relief he was there. She was hanging on the edge of her seat, waiting for what he had to say.

He came forward as a young man but showed himself hiding in his room. The room looked like the lights had been turned off, and he was in isolation, just listening to music. She confirmed that that was a typical day for him. He shared how he didn't want to be pushed, nor really looked forward to growing up. She confirmed that he never wanted to continue school as he resisted growing into his new life. It came out that he ended his life before he had the chance to go off to college, and he secretly did not want to go.

His mom cried into her hands, upset about the fact that she felt like she pushed him too hard. She wanted so badly for her son to grow into the man she saw him to be - creative, imaginative, funny and unique in who he was. But her son wasn't interested in participating in life. He romanticised death and even showed me the eerie tattoos he had on his arm. She confirmed that he talked about death often, but more in a dark kind of way. She felt that because he didn't say he wanted to die and she didn't read the signs of him being actually suicidal, she was hard on herself for his death.

Her son, in spirit, shared that if he wanted help, he would have admitted he was suicidal, but instead, he kept it to himself because he genuinely didn't want to be here. He had no intention of growing into a man and wanted to die before he had to grow up and get a career.

This crushed his mother, whom I felt such huge compassion for. As well as being the medium for her son in spirit and understanding his situation, I felt things as he saw them when I blended my energy with his spirit. It's like empathising with the way they feel and their views. It's a glimpse through their world, and in those moments, everything makes sense.

She felt relief knowing he was okay, but she had a question for him…. She asked me if she could ask him if he regretted dying, seeing how much he had hurt the family.

As she asked the question out loud, I shifted back into his energy to listen deeply for his answer. What he shared through feeling was that he felt no regrets for ending his life but did wish he had found ways to express himself more when he was alive. He realised he had spent so much of his life looking at the dark side, focusing on what was wrong with life, that he never actually found the treasured gifts he was given to use in his life.

I shared with his mom that I felt he had an untouched artistic ability. She confirmed that when he was a child, she felt he was going to be an artist because of the way he drew and his sensitive nature. But her son never followed through on that. He had such a dark sense of humour, but that side never got expressed in art. He shared that his depression took over, and his fascination with death enthralled him. In that obsession, he never really lived. He never noticed what abilities he came in with or what he was even meant to do with his life. He was too busy trying to get out of this life, finding ways to numb it, that he never really lived it.

His mother was happy to hear that he was good with where he was and that he had begun to realise what she had always seen in her son - his special talents, gifts and unique way of seeing life. She was also sad that he never got to use it.

Her son in spirit said that now that he was in spirit, he could understand more what his life was about and that he did miss a lot of what life was trying to offer him by choosing to see the glass half-empty instead of half-full. Because of this perspective, his whole world closed, but he continued growing on the other side where he felt the love all around him.

His mom felt grateful for him coming through and sharing that. She felt peace but still wished he could have been here to live his life. But she also said she would use his words about self-expression and finding his gifts to help her live more of her own life. She was experiencing so much pain now that he was gone, but she knew that if she continued to look at her life with what was missing, she would miss out on what life was trying to give her.

I told her I felt that was a beautiful expression and a great way to live out his legacy. It's good to remember we all come here with gifts, talents and abilities. It's up to us to find ways to express ourselves, as sometimes that is the hidden treasure to finding and appreciating this life. Life is sweeter when you can share your self-expression through your own eyes.

The Dance with Anger

"If you try to get rid of fear and anger without knowing their meaning, they will grow stronger and return."-
Deepak Chopra

Julie came into my office. She asked for spiritual counselling after the loss of the mother she wished she had. Her own mother had died the year before, and, with the loss of both moms in her life, she was finding herself to be angry. She didn't like this anger. It was coming out at work and within relationships. She found that much of it was coming out of nowhere because of all her grief.

Being someone who was quite self-aware and self-responsible and who follows Spiritualism as a way of life and spiritual path, she wanted to find ways to deal with it instead of stuffing it down or lashing out.

We talked about the triggers and the feelings of injustice, of how, in grief, when you lose a loved one, things become real, really fast. The preciousness of life becomes more apparent. To waste days and time doing things you don't want to do feels wasteful and almost inappropriate. Life was waiting, and the trigger of doing things out of alignment or watching people waste their lives is just more aggravating than you may realise.

Grief includes a dance with anger. It cannot be bypassed. It IS part of the process. It is a way for you to claim your power back or fuel you to change when channelled appropriately. Anger will show you where you are not being your authentic self when you let it. It will show you things that are no longer tolerable in your life. It will show you where you are stuck and give you the power to make changes where necessary. The most important is to breathe it through, find the gift in it and let the anger be a motivator to make those necessary changes in your life once and for all.

Movement is a powerful medicine because it gets you unstuck and breaks up the energy. Anger can sit in your belly like fire. When left undigested, it can lash out and hurt the ones you love or make a fool out of you (like giving someone the finger in traffic or yelling at a service worker for slow service.)

I shared with Julie that the best way to move anger is through movement. Put on some upbeat loud music, and move your body, letting it move however it needs, as unattractive as needed. Stick your tongue out like in Lion's Breath in yoga, and move around on the floor. Flick your hands to release energy and let the energy shake out of your body and spine. After about 10-15 minutes, there is a good possibility it will start to release. When you feel tired, lay on the ground and play something soothing. Let the tears fall, or not. But now that your body has moved, it will want the contrast of being still and relaxed. You may have the best meditation you've had in weeks now that you let your body move out whatever was in the way of itself.

One thing to understand about anger is that it's not bad. No feelings are bad, it's just energy trying to move. When you judge them, make them wrong, or try to make them go away, they get bigger and life can go sideways. Grief is like a tidal wave, not always aware of when it will hit, but a crashing wave moving through your body, reminding you just how much you loved. Anger can be an annoyance or that out-of-control feeling you have of life not being fair and the injustice of it all. But this is your time to pray. To shout out to the divine and ask for help.

"Hey Creator! I am miserable here. HELP ME!"

It will be when you are at your mercy, truly surrender, you let help in.

You do not have to try and tough your way through it, for the body does not lie. Try not to let the anger harden you. Grief can open your heart in ways you can't even comprehend. Only when you give yourself permission to express will you find the hidden treasure, as there is always a gift in grief. You have to dive deep to awaken it. There are creative gifts, spiritual gifts, and an opening just waiting for you. Do not rush it, but be there for yourself. It will come in its own timing. In the meantime, be there for you.

Health As A Medium

"When we create peace and harmony and balance in our minds, we will find it in our lives."- Louise L. Hay - *You Can Heal Your Life*

When I first started developing my mediumship and offering it as a service, I was surprised at how many people thought I was putting my health in danger. There seemed to be this belief that all mediums had terrible health, were either really underweight or way overweight, and died prematurely. I definitely had to learn to find that balance and still do.

I walked into mediumship with such a calling, it was a burning desire that wild bulls could not hold me back from. I didn't only want to be a medium, I **needed** to be a medium. It fed me in ways that nothing else did. And quite frankly, my life was falling apart without a deeper calling. One of my medium friends and I would joke that doing a good mediumship reading was like what we imagined a shot of heroin would be. But both of us agreed that there was nothing like it. NOTHING. Doing a meaningful, evidential sitting with someone who had lost their loved one and being able to bring through comfort, connection, closure, and a sense of peace was the greatest feeling and high we had ever experienced before. No matter what else we did in life, there was just no comparison to the shot of love we received and the sense of purpose we felt when we did it.

When I started doing mediumship, I wasn't used to working in such a high vibrational state of love. I just closed my eyes and set an intention, and then I'd be met with a loved one in spirit. Over and over I would do this, sharing messages, giving evidence, and then my nervous system got revved. I stopped sleeping, and I started to feel like my head would explode. Within months of offering my work to the public, I realised I had no idea how much energy this was taking from me, nor did I know how to shut it off once I opened up. This left me feeling wired, tired and chronically ill with a headache or migraine. I felt these energy surges running up and down my body (I know now as kundalini energy). I would take deep breaths to try to calm it, but I had no idea what was happening to me.

This was addressed when I went to England for the first time at the Arthur Findlay College. I was kind of like Harry Potter getting his wand for the first time. I had all this pent-up energy, all this love and passion to do this work, but no sense of control over the spirits coming through. It was controlling me. The best visual I have for myself is a firehose on full blast, flying around with the tap fully on. My energy was vibrating and moving fast, but my body was fatigued, like a wet noodle. My energy was wired, but my body was tired. Which I now know as overloaded.

I didn't get it, how could something I love so much cause me so much pain? How could something I finally found a complete passion for hurt me so bad? My community was starting to wonder how I would keep this up, seeing me dive straight into burnout, but when I got to the college, I was given the grounding and integration I needed.

When I returned home after that first time, I started to recognise more that mediumship was a gift from Spirit, but it was up to me to treat it like a gift. This meant I had to nurture it, care for it, give it time to open and not over-exploit it. I had to learn boundaries, say no more than I said yes, and learn how to open and close it with intention, grounding my energy and knowing how to shut off. Over time, I learned to take more breaks or work in short sprints and balance it with other activities. I found that I came into harmony with mediumship when I remembered I had a physical body and needed to be embodied and not have my head in the spirit world all the time. I realised that 1 hour of designated focused time on mediumship was equivalent to 4 hours of working. So, 2 hours a day was my workday, giving me the same level of work satisfaction as an 8-hour workday.

I have had to face many health challenges for myself, and because of mediumship, I need to be more aware of them (it heightens everything). Being in my body, feeling everything fully gives me the capacity to really be tuned into anything out of alignment. For me, overeating and oversensitivity have always been the reoccurring themes. Eating, for me, was a way to stay grounded and feel a sense of comfort. I have had to shift my relationship with food and have learned to honour my sensitivity by giving myself a lot of downtime and space. With this, I have come to a more balanced life with better health.

Often, when mediums get ill, I believe it's because they are burning themselves out with over-giving, over-revving their nervous system, over-empathizing, people-pleasing and underlying health conditions they already need to be aware of. Mediumship has a way of intensifying your life as you become more sensitive. As you heighten your senses, you become more attuned to your surroundings. When you heighten your sensitivity and learn to read vibration through your nervous system, it is common to touch pain points in your body to let you know and remind you of your limits. Your ability to hold the power will increase over time as you become more attuned to the frequency. But, like anything, you must learn how to build up to it. Where I see mediums hurt themselves is when they try to hold a mediumship reading longer than they are capable of holding the connection to Spirit, which gets them pulling information instead of naturally letting it flow to them. They start to drain their own energy. This is why mediums become so drained and exhausted.

Mediumship done properly should be energising and increase your sense of joy. After all, you are connecting to a power greater than yourself that's a high vibration. But it happens in sprints, not long marathons all at once. It requires balance, and too much of anything isn't good.

Over time, your capacity to hold the power will increase, but get to know your limits from the beginning. Remember to exercise, walk in nature, hydrate, clear your head with meditation, sit in the power and focus on healthy eating to feed and nourish your body. There is no reason you need to suffer or sacrifice yourself to do mediumship. That is old-school thinking that does not need to come into the 21st century. It is completely possible to be a balanced medium who is highly sensitive as well as enjoys working for Spirit but also balances it out with other activities and passions in life. Too much of anything isn't good for you. Always remember that you are in control of your body and it's up to you to take care of it.

Trusting Your Gut

"You don't blast a heart open," she said. "You coax and nurture it open, like the sun does to a rose."- Melodie Beattie

The longer I have been doing mediumship, the more I have realised that there will be times when my clients will trust me more than they trust their physician, psychiatrist, dentist, lawyer, detective, realtor or financial planner. It can be quite overwhelming, but when I really think about it, it's NOT ethical. Of course, in the work I do, we help people trust their nudges or mirror back to them where they have doubts. We help them see where they are stuck and where opportunities lie. This work is about empowerment, helping people see what they can't see, and bringing messages from loved ones that are comforting and healing.

Whenever I talk to my students and they ask me for help because a client asked them something and they felt uncomfortable, they don't always realise it's because the question is crossing a line. It's like this instant feeling of I've got to get away, a sense of dread in their stomach, or dancing around the question and trying not to answer it.

There are many times when people believe those with this ability have an all-seeing eye, but what they don't always know is that it doesn't mean it's for them to share. Often, we hear about spiritual leaders who told their followers they didn't need medical intervention because of mind over matter or they just needed a spiritual healer to heal them.

People have to take responsibility for themselves and their lives and recognise that their medium or physic is not always the best person to consult before a serious matter. Instead, they can be a guide to assist people in finding the answers that resonate with them.

In the past, I have been placed in uncomfortable situations where I did not want to answer someone's question nor had any understanding of what was happening (by my lack of comprehension of the subject, for example, in something like law). But I felt like I had to help, only to realise that it was way out of my zone to even talk about that. Nowadays, I am able to spot the situation quicker, relying on my gut check of *"this is out of my zone"* and being able to let someone know that I am not a doctor, lawyer, accountant, etc. I let them know that I am here to help assist them and that I specialise in reading energy. Often, when people want you to tell them what to do with their lives, they are not trusting themselves or their practitioner, who has a deeper understanding or specialty. They lack trust, so they feel powerless and out of control. It's best to stay grounded in these situations and assist in grounding your sitter as you look at their situation and see how it's unfolding.

So, when a client does come into my office and tries to get me to diagnose them, I can say, *"I talk to dead people, remember? I am not a doctor!"* Sometimes, that remembrance shakes people out of what they were asking. Once the seriousness is out of the room, information can appear that can usually guide the person back to themselves so they can again trust the direction they are going.

I had a student come to me feeling like she couldn't do this work because she was placed in uncomfortable situations. The situation she explained is something I have felt uncomfortable with as well. It's when a loved one passes away, and a person comes to see the medium in hopes they can tell them who's to blame for their death. They hope the medium can do some detective work to bring answers so they can go to the police and charge the person who they believed was responsible for their death. Even though this situation is very serious and needs to be addressed, it is not a medium's job to nail every drug dealer. In fact, in many situations I have experienced, as well as my students, those who pass this way usually express through their messages that they take accountability for their death because they were the ones who took the substance willingly in the first place. This is understandably not easy to hear. And, of course, this isn't the case in every situation.

In mediumship, remember that if you get that sudden feeling of ick in your stomach or feel under pressure to answer a question you don't feel you should answer, always feel free to tell someone that you feel it's out of your scope of practice, or that you don't feel comfortable looking into that for them. You are in control, you get to decide what you will and won't do without judgment. Don't let other people push you around. Your mediumship is your sensitivity, so when situations are heightened or make you feel uncomfortable to answer, you shouldn't. You don't need to stress yourself out to get certain information, not to mention that's usually when you get it wrong anyway. Being under pressure as a medium is the quickest way to get in your head about it. That is not where higher guidance comes from. It comes from your senses.

The Power Of Three

I encounter mediums who never feel like their work is good enough. There is a perfectionism that comes into play with the pressure to keep up to the never-ending high standard they put themselves to. Even though this can be great for striving for more, I also see mediums who break at the first sign of a person not seeing them in their greatness. They crumble away, hoping to hide so they do not have to be seen again in the light of failure. They will do multiple great readings, then they do one that goes sideways, and it just doesn't work - it doesn't go deep enough, or it just doesn't click. The thing about mediumship is you're working with your sensitivity. It takes 3 to make a mediumship reading work. You as the medium (to prepare your vessel), the spirit world (their willingness to bring the information that's needed forward) and the client (has to be open.) You can't be too open to the point they are gullible or too closed off to the point they are cynics. Negativity has a way of closing the reading down, and it has an air of nothing ever being good enough.

Being a healthy sceptic is a good way to be in a reading. It means you are open to the experience, but you will also not believe everything that comes through without evidence. Staying open to the evidence allows a story to unfold in spirit communication. Through keeping an open mind, spirit is more than willing to prove it's really them and the existence of the afterlife.

Sometimes, the person and the medium don't click. Just like in life, there are people we love, people we like, and others where just the sight of them tenses your body without explanation. This can be difficult for the medium. They are usually highly sensitive, empathic people and their very nature is that they want to be liked and get along with everyone.

Sometimes, there is behaviour that doesn't mesh. You think you're speaking English to them, but they hear another language. Whatever you say, they don't hear you, or the way you say it doesn't make sense to the person. It doesn't always fall into place, and in a reading, this becomes intensified. Not to mention that whatever unhealed wounds the medium may be facing in their life, they will meet an edge of inability to help if they are triggered.

Sometimes, the client comes too soon for a reading, and it just isn't time for the spirit communication to come through, or the person receiving is too set on what they want (expectations) or demanding that it doesn't allow room for the flow to happen.

In a reading, the medium nor the client is in control of what happens, but they can set an intention. Spirit's intelligence gets to decide how it will unfold and what to bring to the medium's awareness. The medium has to be trusting enough of the intelligence at play to bring through what's needed in the order that it needs to come in, as spirit has the overview. The medium's job is to empty their mind and open their sensitivity until something happens. The medium can best serve the client by encouraging them to stay open to the experience, and spirit's job is to deliver what is needed. Yes, we are here to serve two worlds (the spirit and receiver), but a medium's job is to get out of the way and allow themselves to become a vessel so spirit can say what's needed at the moment.

The energy that gets created in a reading does take over. When someone comes in with a negative mindset, sometimes the energy gets intensified. The medium's job is to stay in a higher vibration and hold their alignment. That is not always what happens.

Over the years of doing readings, I can honestly say there were readings where I have truly changed people's lives, brought peace to people who were suffering, and turned a sceptic into a true believer. But some readings the chemistry between my client and I was just not a match. But you have to be okay with not being perfect. You will do your best, but sometimes your best isn't going to be as comparable to that time when you first got home from a spiritual retreat. You may strive for perfection, but that is not really the goal, it's showing up and doing your best every day. To prepare your vessel, to strive for better in your self-growth, and even when you fall, to pick yourself back up. To realign, to learn from the failures, to put it into practice again and to keep going.

So, when you do fall, you can sit with that and ask yourself what you could do differently or better in the future.

This is what true humility is. Falling, seeing your part in it and getting back up and doing it again. Always self-improving and never letting an obstacle pull you down. Never let just one reading ruin you as a medium. Never give it that much power. Don't let it take over and dictate the course of your mediumship service, as it will always be changing and evolving anyway. Just when you start to get too comfortable or think you figured it out, that is usually when it happens. Mediumship has a way of keeping you on your toes and inspiring growth as a person and a medium.

At the end of the day, you work for Spirit. You must be willing to let go of what you think needs to happen and surrender to the process that is unfolding. We live in a universe of perfect order; there are no mistakes just learning experiences. We are synced in the tapestry of life and are all connected. Even if things come out of your mouth that you wish you never said, you can always own it and try again. Recognise when things happen, sometimes it is to trigger another, to awaken something that needed to be said, even if it sounded sharp. Sometimes, it was the tone you used that woke someone up to really hear you. Especially when they have been told this many times but refused to listen. You may say it in a way that makes them hear you.

You can choose to see every life experience from a higher perspective. You cannot take responsibility for someone else, but you can do it for yourself.

Chapter 8: Infinite

~

Do You Chose Your Death And When You Die?

June 2016

MAID:

They passed the Medical Assisted Death (MAID) law in BC, Canada. Even though this was seen as progressive by many in our province, there were still many places in the world where this was illegal, especially in our neighbouring country, the USA. I noticed in the spiritual communities, there was a lot of unease around it. Spiritual texts or teachers talked about how this wasn't considered natural, God's plan, or even a quick way out of life. We came in with a reason and would be sent home when we were complete. Some religions were against it, and some were indifferent.

At the time, I watched shows and listened to podcasts about how our culture is allergic to death. We don't honour our elders like we used to and give people good deaths. Instead, we look for a quick fix. There was also the political view that

MAID was a quick way to empty the hospitals and have turnover. It felt cold and disheartening to see the way our medical system treated people.

I could see all angles of this. I heard my nurse friends express their unease about it while hearing other friends talk about how it was great to give the power to the people back and put their death back in their hands.

I remember when my grandfather was sick with a brain tumour for many years. He felt like he had lost all dignity in his illness. He lost his voice and his ability to walk. He went blind and was bedridden for many years. He would have done anything to have something like MAID to end his suffering. He wanted to die for many years, as his brain may have been alert, but his body wasn't. I often thought about that when I heard strong opinions or judgements. How could we really know? Could we really follow spiritual teachers or dated text to know what was best for each person?

So, instead of having a view about it when people asked me my professional opinion, I said I would let them know what the loved ones in spirit say as they come through now that this service is available in BC.

When clients come, I am clear that I don't want details about their loved ones who have passed away. I want them to bring through the information and for the client to validate either a 'yes, no, or 'I'm not sure' as an answer. Having them answer helps build the energy. I think of this like a phone -

they give me the information, I pass it to them, and they answer.

One day, about three days after having this thought about MAID, a woman came to see me for a reading. She wanted to speak with her loved ones in spirit, hoping one specific would come through. I closed my eyes, tuned in and opened up to the light around me. Very quickly, without even a moment to wait, a space filled with light on my left-hand side. It was a feeling of a very excited mother. I shared this information with my client, saying that I felt I had her mother here, and she was overly excited about communicating, letting her know she made it. She was happy, and I told her I felt her mother was new to spirit, like really new. She validated that she had only been gone a few weeks.

Her mother shared a bit about who she was: a strong, independent woman ahead of her time, very communicative, and loved to share knowledge and teach. She confirmed the information. I then said to her, *'Your mom wants me to share she felt very empowered by her death and that she made the right choice and has no regrets.'*

Her daughter smiled. Tears filled her eyes, and the whole room lit up with light and love.

Her daughter shared that her mom was one of the first people to pass of MAID in BC after they passed the law here in our province. She wasted no time and got approved immediately after the law was passed. She had been worried about the afterlife results. She was spiritual, as was her mom, and she was curious to know how it went for her crossing over.

Her mother then shared that she didn't feel her death was unnatural, but in a way, it was always a part of her soul plan. That there was no other way for her. She thought this was how she was always supposed to pass and was paving the way for others to do the same. Not to mention, her mom's personality was to be an early adopter of things. She enjoyed going first and giving reviews!

Her daughter was pleased, especially because she didn't have to ask about her death, and her mom just brought it up. She felt complete that day and could stop worrying about her mother. She could trust her mom made the right decision for herself, and any other teaching, religious belief or point of view could be put aside. She heard it from her mother herself, and that is all that mattered. Her mother felt empowered and said she was fine.

Over the following weeks and years, quite a few other loved ones in spirit came through with similar messages to pass along to their loved ones left behind. All with very similar messages:

- they had a beautiful passing
- they were here one minute and gone the next
- they wouldn't have had it any other way
- it was empowering
- they got to say goodbye

- they don't remember suffering.
- they died with everyone they loved all around them.

The messages kept coming through. It was being validated over and over again. They knew what was best and that was all that mattered.

Not to mention, there is no judging God. There is nothing to be punished or blamed for, as God never judged you in the first place. Maybe doing MAID was the way home for your loved one in spirit. There was never another way. This was how they were always supposed to go. Who are humans to say they weren't given a proper transition?

During the pandemic, I had a man, Eric, contact me while in the hospital with his daughter present. We connected on Zoom, and he asked if we could do spiritual counselling.

I asked him what was going on for him, and he shared that he had been spiritual most of his adult life. He was a huge fan of Delores Cannon, had read all of Sylvia Brown's books, followed astrology, and wanted to do things right. He shared that he spent his whole life doing the right thing. He didn't lie, steal, or cheat. When he was wrong, he promptly admitted it. He cleaned up his messes. He had gotten sober 20-plus years ago and did his best to live his life fully. But he was very sick. So much that he couldn't move much and, as the days progressed, he would lose his memory. He felt like a burden to his daughter, who was a mother, wife, and full-time working woman. He thought he couldn't let her take care of him like this much longer, and being in the hospital was too lonely for him. He felt isolated in his pain, and he wanted to know my professional opinion about MAID.

I shared with him that I could not give him my opinion from spiritual beliefs but would share with him what loved ones in spirit have come through and said directly. He told me he was curious to know.

I told him that in my experience as a medium, without knowing the connotations of how loved ones in spirit died if they passed away from MAID, they usually shared with me that they felt empowered in their passing. That they got to do it their way. They got to say goodbye and that it was a peaceful passing.

Eric took this in and smiled. He liked that answer, he said. *"Am I going to be punished, though?"* He wondered if he was shortchanging his life. Wondered if he wasn't fulfilling his life purpose until that last breath when God took him home.

I let Eric know that that was up to him and the Creator. That there is no judging God. That is a manmade belief, as God is only love, so there is nothing to judge in the first place. However, this was something he would have to take to his prayers and meditation. To ask if he was complete in life and if he passed this way if it was the right decision.

Eric agreed he'd do this. He liked the idea of taking it to the Creator. He recognised in life that when he did wrong things, there was always this feeling of life going sideways. But when he did good deeds in life, those things flowed.

We ended the call. In the end, I told him, *"You know, Eric, I am really happy we had this conversation. When you do pass, please come to me and let me know how it goes for you. I will be very curious."*

Eric promised he would, *"No problem, Nicole. I will call you when I get there."*

Two months later, I did a Zoom call with his daughter. When I got on the call with her, she was already teary. I knew immediately that Eric had passed. She didn't say much when she got on the call, indicating she knew I knew why she was there. As I stared back at her on the Zoom screen, I could see her father standing behind her in glee, illuminating with light.

"Tell her I'm well. Really, really well."

I told her I saw him standing behind her and that he was more excited about this call than she was. He was there to let her know he made it. He was well, and he was happy again. That was all she needed to know and all she had wanted from the reading. Comfort, knowing he was okay and that he was there standing with her.

As I hung up the call after our session, I still felt Eric with me. He was a presence standing on the right side of my body. It was a feeling of being blinded by the light. It was as if a sunray was shining on me through a window, and I had to squint because the light was so bright.

I felt Eric say my name. *"Nicole, I am doing just fine."*

I smiled as my whole body turned to goosebumps. *"Thank you for the confirmation, Eric. I really needed that."*

He smiled back at me, and then I felt him absorb back into the light.

Bargaining With God

"Whatever life takes away from you, let it go."- Don Miguel

Do we choose our own death? Do we have a say in when we die? It's an individual basis, meaning I have had experiences in my life where I have gotten to choose. I have also heard stories from people who felt they had a choice in the matter. Yet, through communication with many loved ones in spirit, I have had many shares about how they don't always get the choice in the matter and that they would have done anything to be able to stay just a little bit longer or say goodbye.

One of my clients shared a story with me over dinner one time. I had done readings for her before, and her father, in spirit, always showed up with her whenever I saw her. He has a presence of just being there and standing over her. In spirit, he told me he had health problems, but he never actually shared about how he died. One evening, when we were out for dinner, she told me she wanted to share with me about how her father had actually passed away. I said to her, *"Oh, didn't he pass of a lung condition?"* She paused and replied, *"No... But let me explain."*

Her father had lung cancer. He had surgery, and during the surgery, he saw himself leaving his body and floating over top of himself while the doctors did surgery on him. He realised he had left his body and was starting to ascend to the other side, but he didn't want to go. He had a family, and they meant more to him than anything else. So, he bargained with God. He asked for five more years; that was all he needed to finish his life. And he did awake from surgery that day. He told his family what happened during the surgery-that he asked for five more years, and he believed he'd get it. From that time, he lived his life fully until it was his official time to go.

Pretty much to the exact 5-year date, her father passed suddenly. Everyone just assumed he would pass from cancer, but he didn't. He passed away from a freak accident by walking into an elevator that wasn't properly hooked in and killed him instantly.

My mouth dropped when she shared this story with me. I could not believe what had happened to her father.

She told me that he passed instantly, and he wouldn't have been in pain. They knew they were gifted those five extra years with him, and all were grateful for that time they had with him. He also continued to help from spirit by directing them to the right people to make sure the elevator got fixed so this incident would never happen to anyone again.

In 2022, my husband Matthew and I came home from Christmas Eve dinner at our friend's house, who lived about twenty minutes away. We decided to leave by 8 pm as we thought the roads would get icy, and we thought we had better leave earlier than later to avoid any issues. We noticed the roads were a bit icy as we drove home, but we took our time and drove slowly. We were on the highway, with its 100km an hour speed limit, going about 70 kilometres around a bend. Suddenly we hit a patch of black ice, and we attempted to realign, only to hit another patch, at which point the car started to spin 360 degrees for about three rotations. At this point, Matthew's hands were off the wheel as there was nothing he could do, and we simply braced, holding each other's hands. Time stood still as we spun down the highway. On the third spin, we hit the crash barrier, then bounced off to turn again. We noticed at that moment that we were literally two metres away from the crash barrier ending and that, as we spun again, there would be no crash barrier to save us as we looked down into a small ravine about ten metres deep. I stated out loud, *"GOD, SAVE US!"* The crash stopped our spinning in one direction, causing us to spin one rotation in the other direction. Thankfully we came to a stop in the middle of the road facing the direction we intended to head.

I looked to my right of where we were headed in that spin, and it was quite the cliff. At that moment, a miracle occurred. We could not save ourselves, but God could. As we got back on the road, driving straight, two elk appeared out of the woods and looked directly at us as they crossed the road.

They felt like an omen, a gift from Spirit to show us our prayers were heard.

We counted our blessings the whole way home as we shook uncontrollably and breathed until we reached our driveway. I got out of the car, expecting to see our car totaled and done in, but there was just one dent and one bump, barely noticeable. But again, we were blessed with no injury, no whiplash, and barely any car damage. Instead of asking, *"Why me, God?"* I stated, *"Thank you, thank you and thank you."* I know many of my friends and people I met in spirit were not always lucky. But then again, not a single one has come to me in spirit and told me their death was a mistake; there is always a plan. There is always a reason why someone is here and someone isn't. Even though we cannot understand it, I know we cannot get in the way. One day, it will make sense, and we will get answers as to why. But until then, the words are *thank you.*

May 2014

There have been times when I have communicated with loved ones in spirit and they have shared that their death was a complete surprise. That they didn't see it coming or feel any warnings. Instead, they had a sudden death and woke up on the other side.

My friend Katie's fiancé was 30 when he went missing while biking in Nova Scotia. After he went missing, there was a huge search for him, looking high and low with the military, trying to locate him. After six days of intense searching, they were unable to find his body. Because of the heavily wooded area, cliffs and abandoned mine shafts, they believed that he must have slipped down the trail off the side cliff and under the ruffage. There was a lot of unacceptance from his family that he could have died, thinking that at any moment he would appear. However, Katie, knowing the area and realising how out of character all of this was, felt in her gut that he had died on the trail. Their wedding was planned just a few months later, and she knew something was seriously wrong when he did not come home that expected evening.

Katie went to mediums, and all were able to identify that they saw a man around her with a bike, who died suddenly by hitting his head. Consistently hearing this information led to Katie's intuition being confirmed, and she knew to believe it. We'd sit and call on his spirit and ask him to communicate with us. His presence in spirit was easy to identify, though something he always shared was that his death was such a surprise. He didn't see it coming and it all happened so fast. He died before he remembered anything, and his spirit left his body. Even though he died in unlikely circumstances, finding his body was not necessary for him.

To this day, his body has never been found. I have shared with Katie that Marty's death was around the time that my mediumistic abilities really started to open. I believe it was because of Marty that I felt the need to further my development as I saw how valuable it was to Katie. She needed that comfort of knowing he was okay in spirit and that she didn't need to do anything further to find his remains. Over a year later, after his passing, we went to a mediumship demonstration together and Marty came through for Katie from the medium. One of the messages she told Katie from Marty was that he wanted her to know that he died suddenly, and then she looked at me and said, "*He says thank you for passing the messages.*" It was heartwarming to hear this and I am grateful that, even from spirit, Marty thought to thank me for developing my mediumship so I could help Katie with his passing and be the messenger between worlds.

What's It Like On The Other Side?

"It's amazing Molly. The love inside you- you take it with you." - From the movie *Ghost*

Each one of our loved ones will have a unique death and departure to the other side. When it comes to the end of someone's life, each person may have a different perspective on the experience and personal beliefs can heavily play in the nature of the transition.

What I do know is that, just like how I know when a child is born, the room is filled with support from the other side all around the birthing mother; it is the same for when our loved ones pass away. Often, a loved one in spirit will show me who was there for them when they passed. Or they won't let go until they are greeted by a loved one in spirit ready to come get them.

Some examples of stories loved ones in spirit have communicated about passing over are:

A bright light filled the room, and I was just gently magnetically pulled into the light.

The room was filled with angels and higher beings. The room became so light and bright as I lifted into their presence. It was glorious and beautiful.

My father woke me in the early morning, standing at the foot of my bed and told me it was my time. I stepped into the light with him.

I didn't even know it happened. If I had known I was dying, I probably would have turned around. I was dreaming, and when I never woke up, I realised I had passed away. It was like a continuation of a dream.

In more tragic scenarios like suicide, overdose or traumatic/painful death:

Everything just went quiet and black. I felt nothing, just a restful sleep. I have no idea how long I was in that state.

I left my body, yet I was still there, standing over my body until the family found me.

I felt a surge of energy like a spiral. As I moved through it, I was greeted in spirit by my loved ones.

I went into a holding space. This was a quiet place where I was wrapped up like a cocoon and just got to rest, recover, and not think about anything.

After I passed away, I was still there. I wanted to help. I wanted to ensure I wanted to ensure everyone was okay until I moved on to the next phase of my journey.

After each soul has their passing and their own unique transition, they may take their time familiarising themselves with where they are. They have to get used to not having a physical body but that they are part of all of life and creation again. Sometimes, this takes a minute to adjust, while others shift quickly.

A friend I knew, Linda Fine, was a medium and a circle friend to many here in the Cowichan Valley. When she passed away, she showed my medium friend Pam Malt who was with her in her transition that she was in the sky and stretched her energy, saying, *"Glory, glory, glory!"* to show how amazing it felt to extend her energy so far so fast. Imagine that all of a sudden you went from viewing with your two physical eyes to being everywhere all at once, seeing everything through many eyes. There is no limit to your expansion and your evolution continues, even on the other side.

Life Review

"In the tapestry of life, we're all connected. Each one of us is a gift to those around us helping each other be who we are, weaving a perfect picture together." - Anita Moorjani

March 2018

I heard about a medicine that was not a pharmaceutical, but a plant medicine called Ayahuasca. It is used in healing ceremonies with shamans in Central and South America. I noticed there was a bit of a fad, a trend going around in North America, where people were becoming increasingly interested in working with these indigenous plant medicines. I heard about it in Cowichan Valley, BC, where I live. I also heard about mediums in Holland and England who were working with the medicine and were finding it was really helping them open up and expand into their mediumistic gifts, and it sparked my interest. At that time in my mediumistic development, I was starting to hit a bit of a pause, as if I could only go so deep in my mediumship. I was starting to wonder if this medicine could help me like it was helping my international friends and acquaintances. Maybe it could help me go a little bit deeper into my work.

Also, one of the things I heard about taking Ayahuasca is that it has the ability to show you other aspects of who you are and understand your life better, as people described it. There is your life before you take Ayahuasca and life after. You are never the same person going in as who you are going out. I had heard stories about people who had taken the medicine and it radically changed their lives. Going from corporate jobs, living in the city, to moving to Mexico to run a surf shop or opening up to their creative gifts, like art, music, writing and even mediumship. I was interested in how my life would change if I took this plant spirit medicine.

I put the thought out there just offering it to the Universe, and within about six weeks, I started noticing that people around me were sharing about an indigenous elder within our community who was offering circles. He was offering this medicine by word of mouth and invitation only. It was someone I had already known for a few years. There were things I guess he didn't share with just anyone and he let you find out through other ways, but any true medicine man is like that; a person of mystery. He had trained under Shamans in Peru and had over 20 years of experience. I approached him about taking the medicine, and he agreed to let me do it. I put a group of friends together and we all did our Deita, which included cleaning up our diets, minds, and lives before taking communion with the plant spirit medicine.

I intended to become a better medium and have a life review. It fascinated me that I could be a different person tomorrow and have a different perspective on my life. I heard about some people's near-death experiences where they would go through a life review. In their experiences, they would get to see their life from another lens, a different perspective, to see how their behaviour had affected others and how their actions had a ripple effect on the world. I was curious how I impacted people, how I got in my own way, and how I could hurt myself and my progression without even knowing it.

Most importantly, I didn't want to wait until I died for this experience. After my close call with death before, I did not want to go through a near-death to have an experience where I realised I really wanted to live. I wanted to be conscious of going through something like this and live each day fully.

So, in Spring, under a Scorpio full moon, I sat with the medicine man as he poured me the tea. It was a thick, dark brown substance that tasted and looked similar to bitter molasses. I looked him in the eyes and stated my intention again in my mind as I downed the drink in one chug. I moved back onto my mat, and I laid down. Within 15 minutes or so, I noticed these geometric shapes forming on the ceiling. We were in complete darkness late at night in a yurt with about 7 of us. The shaman started to sing Icaros, songs to activate the spirit of the medicine. Within half an hour, he invited us up to his mat one at a time to sit in front of him as he sang us specific Icaros to activate our journey. Something he was guided to as the holder of the medicine to put us on our journey for the evening.

When he invited me up, I rolled over on my mat and tried to stand on two feet to walk over to him, but I realised I couldn't. The medicine was too strong and was grabbing a hold of me already. I looked down at my body and saw that I had shapeshifted into a large cat. I crept up to him on all fours, sitting in front of him upright and strong, like any cat would greet someone. He started to sing this chant directly to me, rattling little bells and shakers around me. I smiled with glee as I bounced along feeling the frequency of the music as it entered my soul. But when I looked at him again, he was no longer the man who had administered me the medicine half an hour earlier. He was now dressed in a giant headdress. These white feathers almost touched the yurt's ceiling and dropped to the floor. There were emerald jewels on his forehead, creating a band over him. His deep chocolate eyes sparkled deeply.

As he looked at me and sang, I started to feel this swirl of energy taking over and beginning to shift my reality. Nausea started to take me, and he grabbed a bucket from beside him and he placed it under me as I puked. I didn't like the feeling that was starting to take over me. It was a feeling of being out of control, like the dosage I took was more than I could handle. Up until this point in my life, I had never taken any psychedelics before, nor did I enjoy being under the influence. In fact, I hadn't consumed any mood-altering substance since I was 20 years old. The sheer panic and fear started to take me as I realised I was not going to be able to control this, that I had to surrender to the experience of letting the medicine take me.

I made my way back to my mat, but the internal spinning in the room was getting too much. I looked around me, and I could see this golden cord of light join me to each person in the room as if I were in a spider web. I started to feel everything everyone else was feeling, and I no longer had a grip on myself. It was too much too fast, and I started to scream bloody murder. I got up immediately, crawling on all fours and trying to reach the door. I ripped open the door, gasping for air as I disconnected from the circle and caught a breath outside in the night. I hated that I became that connected to everyone. I hoped to God that when I got out of this yurt, the feelings of nausea would go away. That the feeling of oneness with everyone in that room would stop.

As I stepped out of the yurt, I attempted to stand up, pacing along the porch from left to right, to centre myself. All of a sudden, I heard this woman's voice that came from outside of me. I now know her as Ayahuasca. She told me, *"This is not about wanting to become a better medium. I will show you how to become a better person. To do that, I must show you everything you have ever judged."* Right then, I broke and fell to my knees. Ayahuasca was going to show me no mercy. She was tough love, and she did not care. She was dedicated to me that night to reveal who I really was, how I affected those around me and how I contributed to my own suffering.

She showed me immediately through imagery and feeling how I had spent my whole life trying to be perfect. If only I could become a little bit better, stronger, and more accurate, then maybe people would stop judging me. But I realised in that moment it was never about them or trying to be anything. I was on a journey of self-investigation to love myself more, to unravel me. I didn't have to be better at anything, but I did need to become more whole in who I was. That night, I could write an entire other book, but I can tell you that I spent about 2 Earth hours (which felt like an eternity). I returned to the very moment of conception and birthed into this realm. I saw myself in the womb. I felt all my mother's emotions. I saw my childbirth, and then I experienced every feeling and emotion I ever had as an infant, and then I started to grow up from that age. I saw every connection, relationship, and judgement that was mine and those others had towards me.

There was no filter while I was in my life review. It was like I was inside a tunnel with many movie screens playing out spontaneously all at once, and I was corded to each screen playing out like a cosmic web. I was spiralling into it and feeling everything. Some emotions were bigger than others, leading to releases of vomit as it let go of me. There was no filters with Ayahuasca. She took me there, and she made me go directly into it and feel it all the way. Every time I felt a projection shoot at me, I vomited. Whenever I saw myself with envy, greed or jealousy, I vomited or dry heaved.

As the night progressed, there wasn't much left, so I let it go however it could leave me. Anytime I felt a moment of love or purity, my heart opened. As I spiralled, which felt like an eternity, my whole life was realised in front of me. I saw how I affected people. I saw how I hid myself, how I kept myself quiet, and how I created barriers and guards so I didn't have to feel and didn't have to be projected at. I saw how, not only people's hurtful feelings of me affected me, but how I affected them, and there was no separation between the two of us. We were all in a tapestry of life. What Ayahuasca gifted me with was the ability to see this before I died. And yes, I did feel like I died to myself that night so that I could be reborn. A part of me felt like this was a near-death experience. Not only because I was screaming out, "*I am going to die! This medicine is too strong! I am sorry you will be shut down tomorrow when the police come to collect my body*", but I guess I did feel like I was dying to go there, to go that deep to have the rebirth.

My life was never the same after this. I saw all the physical ailments I carried and why I had them. I saw how my self-projections were keeping me ill. I also discovered I had to be kinder to myself. My mediumship didn't have anything to do with this. But the more I learned to fall in love with myself, the more I opened, and the more I became vulnerable and truthful while still keeping my feet on the ground. It allowed me to be more truthful about who I was, and within that, my mediumship became a natural expression, and I took the pressure right off me.

As the days passed after the ceremony, I started integrating and developing artistic abilities. I began to open and bloom into new creative gifts. I started a large cat collection of paintings of jaguars and lions, realising and discovering these hidden talents and abilities I had under the surface that were longing to come out. There was more power within, and I became more mindful of my blueprint and my actions in this world. After having such a clear view of every action I created and was a part of, whether it left my mind of thoughts or not, I had an imprint, a ripple effect, and I no longer doubted that.

Would I recommend this medicine to everyone? Is Ayahuasca the Holy Grail to discovering your true self? It's one way but not the only way. Over the years, I have found other ways to unveil my true self that are less harsh and invasive. But I do credit these powerful medicines and how they can wake people up from their illusions of life. For me, it was just the medicine I needed at that time. These days, I prefer a much gentler way of getting there through grace. But I can recognise when plant spirit medicines are necessary, and I reverently respect these plant allies. I also know that the medicine calls you, and as much as I thought I called the medicine to me, I believe I was placed and was called to the medicine. These plant medicine allies are powerful and potent. I don't believe you need to search far and wide to get to them. If you are meant to be working with them, it will show up just around you and the perfect time in your life to align with you. And with your intention, it will take you where you need to go to discover your true self, and it will show you in a way that will humble and ground you like nothing else in this world will.

Feeling It All

"You don't have to try to be good; you just need to stop pretending to be what you are not." - Don Miguel

       The only way you can know an emotion in another is if you have felt that within yourself first. You cannot be afraid to feel it, for it grows into wisdom. As a medium, you learn to become attuned to vibration - it's recognisable invisible energy. This is how you can hold space for another person: you have felt the emotions that they are going through and understand them. You have to have been there yourself emotionally or have a deep compassion for their situation and experiences.

Often, where mediums get stuck or plateaued is when they can't feel and freeze up. They have met an edge as deep as they have been within themselves. Sometimes, situations can trigger, make them pause in what they are doing, space out, or something not so spiritual may come out of their mouth (a projection).

There is continuous learning and growing in your life and your mediumship development. You never arrive as a medium, you will keep evolving, opening the doors to more.

The deeper you go within, the more that will unfold in your communication through knowing, sentience, and just feeling the spirit communicator closely. This is why spiritual healing is important when working with energy. To receive and give healings helps you become attuned to allowing spirit to work through you in this way. It will help you know thy self, to be able to hold space and be there for someone else. Otherwise, it may come out as judgment.

You will notice that some mediums can describe what they see but don't always know what it means. To understand the messages being communicated from spirit, it's important to let them in and feel it. It would be best if you felt so deeply that what is being shown clairvoyantly can be felt and transmuted into a piece of evidence or message. Mediumship communication is so much more than just sharing visions. It is alive and transmutable. Seeing spirit is one thing, communicating spirit through all senses is a whole new level. It's a living language.

As you develop yourself as a medium, you will meet that point in your life where you are being asked to feel things that you may not have been able to before. Through life experiences such as personal loss, career growth, health conditions, or moments of deep empathy, your wisdom will grow. Not only in your own life, but in your understanding and communication with spirit. Spirit is more than willing to teach and guide you. Know that there is nothing to fear because as you grow and expand your capabilities, you are only deepening your understanding of self.

The Ripple Effect

"Despite how open, peaceful, and loving you attempt to be, people can only meet you as deeply as they've met themselves." - Matt Kahn.

Who you are as a person will greatly affect who you are as a medium. You cannot separate a person from their natural expression of mediumship. It is an aspect and expression of your soul. This work is precious, guided by Spirit and is meant to be used for service to others. Over the years, as you develop your connection, your relationship will evolve and change, bringing you closer and in more contact. As with any relationship you nurture in life, it can be enriched with care and dedication.

It's a common occurrence that I get asked if mediumship is just a phase for me or if I will be evolving into greater things where I will graduate from communing with loved ones in spirit and move on to higher beings in the future. The honest answer is, I don't know, I don't really care, and as long as it feels right, I will continue doing it in the way that Spirit brings it to me, as there is no real "higher work" anyway. Now, of course, there are different aspects of mediumship that I am interested in, but they ebb and flow. The world is constantly evolving, and so am I as I move with it. Sometimes, my writing is more of an expression (like in writing this book), or my art takes the front stage. Sometimes, I go deep into teaching, enriching my skills and development as a teacher to help others with their development. Sometimes, my evidential mediumship takes the front stage, or deeper communing with my guides and healers in spirit form feels like my new purpose. Maybe because my intention is to allow Spirit to express itself through me, I feel called to different work at different times. Still, I never want to pigeonhole who I am or what I do, as Spirit is limitless, and I have developed such a trusting relationship with the divine that if I were guided to do something else, I simply would.

The base of this work is around the power of love and how love heals. It's a reconnection to family beyond the veil. The more you dive into it, the more you realise the sole purpose of this work is to bring healing, comfort and meaning to this world. If your loved ones in spirit see you suffering, they will try their best to get ahold of you to bring support and help from on the other side.

The ripple effect of mediumship is more than anyone can truly comprehend, as there is no agenda to it. It's love in action, in the moment and fluid. Being a channel for spirit has allowed me to clean up relationships in my life, become more forgiving and open, and keep my feet on the ground as well as continuous evolvement. Spirit has no limits, and there is no ending to our evolution.

Right now, with where we are in humanity, there is a heavy influence from technology. This may have to do with the Age of Aquarius (element is air) and the use of technology growing in our modern world, but spirit working in union with this instead of against it. Spirit is learning to use technology to communicate and find ways to reach us. I can't tell you how many times things have happened on my phone where my iTunes music has turned on out of the blue and played a meaningful song with a message. Or a memory picture shows up on my phone of a loved one who has now passed on who I was thinking about in my head that second. Or Siri popping on out of nowhere, saying something that answers a thought to a question. Or things pop up that I need to know that I can also take as a sign. You can call that clever marketing, but you cannot deny that a merging and blending is going on with spirit and technology. Even though it can be scary to see where that could take us, I remain optimistic and pray that good can come out of it, too. As what you focus on grows, I may as well choose to see the benefits.

I am so grateful I can stay in touch with some of my best friends overseas who also practice mediumship because of forms of communication in technology and all the online classes that are now being taught. It was only pre-pandemic that people were still hesitant that we couldn't learn mediumship in online classes or do readings over the internet. But of course, Spirit has proven that that is a non-issue, only we are slow to realise they cannot be limited. Spirit is everywhere and that includes the internet.

I am excited to see what is down the pipeline for mediumship in its revolution, as I know people are more open and receptive to this work than even ten years ago. It is becoming mainstream and normal to have in conversation. It no longer has to be about overcoming witch-burning conversations and secret circles hidden away, but spirit work is open and in the public.

The most important thing about all this work is the connection to love. If you feel called to be of service in this way, open your hands and let Spirit guide you, as Spirit will be your greatest teacher and most guided force. Have intentions, but keep them light, as you will be guided to places, people and things you have never considered. The work you will do for humanity will have a ripple effect, as the creator's natural state of energy is in abundance. When you open to that flow of energy and receive, more will come back to you in ways you have never imagined. Every act of love is noticed in the divine creation, as that is the only thing that is truly real in our universe. So, when you wake in the morning and are guided by your day, let love be your guiding force, as love leads the way. Every. Single. Time.

Chapter 9: Religion

~

Religious Interference

"Remember that when you leave this earth, you can take with you nothing that you have received - only what you have given." - Saint Francis of Assisi

Spring 2021, and a man came to me for a mediumship reading. He wanted to tell me all about his loved one in spirit who passed away, but before I gave him a chance to tell me anything, I asked him if he could stay quiet, let me bring through the information and see what Spirit had to say.

It was his wife, and a beautiful woman she was. She shared all about her charm, spitfire personality and how much she was a people person. She shared about her husband being the love of her life and how they were from the East Coast of Canada. He cried throughout the reading, telling me he just had to know she made it. He just HAD to know she was okay, that she made it to Heaven, and all was well with her.

He shared how they were both religious, but when they moved out west, they stopped practising their religion.

It was a lovely connection, and never for a moment did I feel doubt from him as the love that came through I felt so real between the two of them.

As the reading wrapped up, I took a moment with him as he wiped his face with tissues. It was a very emotional reading, and he took a deep breath and leaned back in his chair. I felt how I usually did after a heartfelt reading - full, inspired and touched by the connection from Spirit.

Suddenly, I noticed when I looked at him that his face changed. He hardened. His brow furrowed and it was like reality was settling in for him of what happened.

I didn't say anything. I just sat there witnessing and holding space for him. I didn't want to get up as I didn't want to rush the experience. I wanted him to feel he had the space to feel fully before he left.

Then he said to me, *"I am not sure how your husband sleeps at night knowing you do the Devil's work in your basement."*

My eyes widened. *"Excuse me?"* I gasped, shocked he went there.

"Yah, this is Devil's work. I don't know how you can live with yourself. This work is prohibited in the Bible."

I gulped but held my alignment. Not for a moment did I want him to feel he had power over me in this moment, nor did I want him to speak like this to me in my own house. *"I wouldn't do this work if I had even one ounce of guilt, even 1/100th if this was wrong. My husband and I sleep quite well at night, knowing I am doing God's work in my basement."* I said back to him boldly.

He shook his head, and his face went red. *"I just don't get it. I just needed to know she made it to Heaven. I know that now. But now I need to go pay my penance for seeing you."* He put his hands over his face to cover it, still glossy in the eyes. He looked ashamed for what he did, coming to see me, but I would not let him pour that shame onto me.

"I have no shame in what I do. In fact, the spirits come to me. I never go looking for them. Hence why I asked you not to talk about your wife as you came in. She came to this reading, in this union together we opened the door." I got up and started walking to the door.

He started tying his shoes but looked away. Then he whispered under his breath, *"But yet I still came. Something made me come here today."*

"That's right. You followed your spirit here. Remember, I don't know you, you found me."

He left, shutting the door behind him. No last words, just a shun from him.

There was not enough sage in the village to smudge my basement that day after he left. I lit a tealight candle for his wife in spirit and prayed to her. I told her I did my job, I was grateful she used me to be her medium and I could represent her, but I prayed he never returned and could find the support he needed. I put my hand over my heart and honoured her. I let the tealight candle burn until completion.

When you do this work day in and day out, it becomes very obvious the difference between spiritual evidence of the afterlife and religious brainwashing.

Religious belief sounds like…

"You will be punished for your sins."
"It is NOT okay to commune with the afterlife. You give it all to Jesus."
"Seeing a medium is a sin; you will pay for it. The Devil disguises himself as fallen angels."

Spirits come in vibration. Energy cannot lie. It just is. Love is love. Shame is shame.

There is nothing unnatural about wanting to feel a connection with your ancestors and loved ones directly. If they didn't come to me or make the link, we wouldn't be doing this. Period.

I was fortunate to have a father who made a point and a stance for me not to grow up in a religious household. We did not attend a church. Family members on my dad's side did. Actually, my grandparents on my dad's side showed concern to my parents that they thought we were all going to Hell because we didn't go to church.

I grew up as a very curious child. I wanted God in my life. I was born with a connection, but it confused me when I was pushed out of friendship circles because I wasn't a Christian or had a religious upbringing.

When I was a teenager, I resented my family for not wanting me to go to church, but I can understand why they felt the way they did. My dad steering me away from religion moved me towards teachings that allowed me to have a direct link to God without feeling guilt or shame because of it. I see many suffer for considering approaching mediumship when their religion has taught them to see it as evil.

Matthew's Grandmother

In September 2021, I had an eye-opening experience of my own in relation to religion that helped me respect religious choices a little bit more.

My husband Matthew's grandmother was 94 when she passed away. She was a devout Catholic and practised most of her life. She was proud to be a Catholic, which served her well. She enjoyed everything about it and would have loved it if Matthew had stayed a Catholic and married a nice girl from church. At our wedding, when we had our spiritual ceremony calling in the directions and honouring our departed loved ones, his grandmother came to me after the ceremony. She said, *"God hasn't forgotten you"*.

I smiled and replied, *"I know."* And left it at that.

When she passed away, we thought she would be one to communicate with us or let us know when she made it. I felt the moment she passed away. I was folding laundry in my sock drawer, and suddenly, I felt a jolt as if something had shifted. I tuned in and noticed that I could no longer see her in her physical body, she was soaring. She had been in hospice for a couple of months, and for about nine days, she was dying. I was able to physically witness her leaving her physical body when we went to visit her. It was like her spirit body was ascending out of her physical body. I watched the energy move around her as if her head was lit up and glowed, but now, energy was moving through the lower half of her body. The way I see it is when people start to die consciously, they leave their body one chakra at a time, working their way up the body. The last time I saw her, she was up to her throat chakra. When I thought of her, I would consciously send her a blessing, as I know many other family members did as well.

But after she died, Matthew and I often talked about whether she would shift her perspective in the spirit world. Would she still be a Catholic? Would she go straight to Jesus? Or would there be a change in perspective of her beliefs? Would it all become one big cosmic joke?

Often, my clients have asked me when their religious or atheist family member would die, would they say, "*You were right!*" I couldn't help but feel there might be a deeper conversation about it after a long period of time, but probably not in the short term if they had any pride.

But we were so curious about what his grandmother would say. When she was dying, she did ask her daughter and granddaughter if her husband would be there or if her sister would. Who would come first was a big question of hers.

So, we waited. Every time I tuned in, I felt like I had someone shutting the door in my face. I accepted that and didn't push it, not even for a second. I thoroughly believe our loved ones in spirit come when they are called to and when they have a message to pass on. But never try and pry or summon the spirits. Just let them come to you.

Her funeral came around mid-week. It was about five days after she died, and as we went to her service, we sat in the Catholic Church and watched the priest conduct the service. There were blessings with holy water, and they blessed it with Frankincense. We prayed, he blessed her, and we all sang hymns. It was exactly what she wanted, and I am so glad her wishes were honoured. As I stared down at the casket and looked up at the priest in his gown, I felt nothing. I didn't feel much emotion. I didn't sense her spirit around, and it felt a little quiet. I thought it was me. Probably because these traditions weren't mine. I wasn't a practising Catholic, and I didn't want to project that onto any of the family, but I was a little surprised that I didn't sense her spirit. Usually, when I was at a funeral or celebration of life, I would feel head-to-toe goosebumps whenever I was there.

After the funeral, we drove to the burial. Again, the priest showed up, blessed the casket, and said a prayer. We all placed some dirt onto the casket as the flowers were laid over. As the ceremony ended, the family took a step back to reflect. All of a sudden, a gust of wind came. It blew through all of us, all at once. I looked up and noticed a shift in the energy. Suddenly, a yellow monarch butterfly came out of nowhere and started flapping its wings as it made its way through all of us. It landed directly on the casket. My heart filled with love, my eyes with emotion. There she was. She waited for the ceremony to be over.

"I was Catholic then, and I am Catholic now!" She spoke into my ears. It was in her voice, like a narrator in the background speaking loudly in her tone.

I chuckled, realising what she was getting at. She wanted her service first. She wanted her blessing to happen before any spirit communication. She needed her Catholic service. Man, do I respect that now. When the funeral and burial were over, she came in full swing. She was here and all around us.

On our car ride home, I shared this with Matthew. We talked about that part of her life where she lived in Africa. I felt she loved living there, but Matthew wasn't sure if she did. Suddenly, on my iTunes playlist, a song called "Spirit" by Chris De Burgh came on, which has African rhythms and specifically mentions not crying for one who has departed. We smiled the rest of the way home. Feeling her with us, feeling her spirit moving through us and in every aspect of our being. She was home.

Weeks later, she came through a medium friend of mine. Without any information about who she was, her message was that she wanted the family to know that when she arrived, a little man was standing there waiting for her. This was her husband. I am so glad she confirmed that, being that that was one of the questions she was asking herself and telling others before she died.

The Slap

I wondered if our loved ones in spirit stay in their religion long-term when they cross over to the other side or if they become more open-minded. I believe now that's an individual choice, and we have the freedom to do what's comfortable for us. Some seem to open their minds a bit more when they crossover, seeing that religion is not a divider, and others stay strong with what they believe.

I was doing a demonstration of mediumship at the Spiritualist Centre. As I got up to demonstrate, I noticed this mother standing with me who wanted to speak with her daughter. She showed me the cross around her neck, the Bible in her hand and that her faith came first, even before her family. I quickly found her daughter in the audience, and she validated that her mother was this and that she chose her religion over being a mom. As I got deeper into the reading, she mentioned how she was too stuck in her way to believe that there was another way to God but that she was still with Jesus as that was her path. However, she was glad her daughter found a spiritual connection.

At the end of the reading, I made a joke that if her mother were alive, she would have for sure thought we were doing the Devil's work. Just as I said that I felt her mother, who was standing with me on my left side, slap me across the face. My face lit up burnt red and started to tingle. It was noticeable something had happened as I started to burn up on stage. I touched the side of my face as I soothed the red-hot surface and tingles, I told her daughter that I believed her mother just slapped me. She gasped as she covered her mouth and laughed while nodding her head.

At the end of the service, the woman came up to me and told me that if anyone ever made a comment about her religion, she would slap them. And that each of her siblings, including herself, got slapped many times in their upbringings for thinking differently than her religion. I apologised if I was disrespectful to her mother, but the woman said, "*No, that was perfect. That was how I REALLY knew my mother was with you.*"

When I drove home that day, I regretted how I handled the situation, thinking I could have been a bit more tactful and could have gone without the joke at the end. But then I realised I would have been getting in the way if I didn't say that. The slap was part of the evidence. It was part of her mother, and it was concrete proof her mother was there and was apologising for choosing her religion over her family.

Even though we may pass and change perspectives on the other side, something I have come to realise over and over again is that we take ourselves with us wherever we go. Evolution of the soul is available to all of us, and it's our choice how much we choose to grow on the other side. But regardless of anything, we take the love we had on Earth forward on our journey.

Chapter 10: Forgiveness

~

The Threads That Join Us

"Forgiveness moves down the ancestral bloodlines of all humanity… dissolving genetic blocks and lifting karmic curses wherever it travels" - Richard Rudd

When my friend Jewleana died, she connected with me through a dream the night I found out about her death. In the dream, I met with her in her home. As we walked through her home, it was filled with mould. I saw all that "old stuff" she was carrying around, and I saw how sick she really was, dying of cancer.

We walked out of her old mould-filled house and into a train cart. We got in, and the cart travelled at the speed of light. It was her life flashing before our eyes. It was too fast for me to make sense of it, but I could tell she was watching her whole life play before her. Then we arrived at a stop. It was real life, and someone was delivering the news of her death to her parents. We watched out the window as they received the news of her death. Jewleana was estranged from her parents for over 25 years. This tortured her every day, and she was unable to make peace with it. As we watched her family being told the news, we saw her mom and dad fall apart crying. Jewleana looked at me and said, *"I've been waiting my whole life to see this."* She wiped the tears from her eyes, and empathetically, I felt that that brought her some closure, knowing they still cared despite the fact they hadn't had a relationship for so long. She turned to me on the train tracks and started to glow.

"Nicole, it doesn't matter what you do or where you go, but who you help along the way." She smiled at me as she said this, then was absorbed into the light and gone in an instant. I woke up with those words repeating in my head. I quickly got up and wrote them down, and I have never forgotten them.

Forgiveness

As a minister, it is quite frequent that I get asked to speak on the topic of forgiveness. Often, this topic will be brought up at a service I give, and I get to speak inspirationally about it.

My friend Lana was chairing for me in fall 2022, and she picked the book *"It Didn't Start with You"* by Mark Wolynn. The chapter she read was on forgiving your parents. After the chairperson reads a passage from a book, I am to stand up and speak inspired on this subject with no previous knowledge of what the subject will be on.

As Lana read the passage from this book, it talked about how healing our relationships with our mother/father is one of the most important things to do on our path of awakening. Choosing to stay closed on this chapter of your life can cause negative effects on us. As Lana read this in the book, I looked around the room. I saw a few people tense up, another start rubbing her neck, and a few in the back mumbling to each other under their breath. I could feel in the field of energy that I was tapped into a very sensitive subject and one that I had to handle delicately. I handed it over to Spirit and asked them to speak through me in a way that could be compassionate and loving, direct and meaningful.

When I stood up to speak I broke the ice by saying I felt I needed a PhD in psychology before taking on this subject. However, as a minister, I witnessed more miracles and healing by handing this over to Spirit than by psychoanalysing it.

When I worked in a residential drug and rehabilitation centre from 2013-2015 I got to be support staff sitting in on sweat lodge ceremonies. In the presence of the elders and continuous prayer, I witnessed more miracles in that lodge, helping people to forgive (by feeling instead of speaking) than I ever saw by people walking in and out of group family counselling.

Every relationship we have in life traces us back to our roots of origin. Essentially, this has us look at our relationship with our mother and our father. I understand that not every child grows up in a loving environment. The negative consequences of having a parent who neglected their child can be life-altering and troubling for people as adults. I also understand that most children long for a connection with their parents, even if it is unhealthy. It is not always about wanting to stay in discord with family but wishing anything but the wall facing them. Sometimes, the only way to love your parents is to hold a boundary and love from a distance. Forgiveness is so much more than saying what happened was water under a bridge and moving on. Forgiveness is about setting yourself free from the burden that is holding you back. It's about unhooking yourself from the way things were supposed to be to allow things be as they are.

As I spoke on the subject of forgiveness that day, I realised there is such a misrepresentation of what forgiveness really means. It's never been about the other person, it's about setting yourself free. You can love someone but not really like them, and that is okay. Learning to keep your heart open but still have boundaries in your life to be there for yourself can be one of the healthiest things you can do for yourself. Forgiveness teaches you to let go of the judgement of what they did and live from your heart, to unhook from the pain and give that love back to yourself. Whenever someone does something to you that you do not approve of, take that as a learning to never do that to someone else.

****

I was at an event doing a group reading for a metaphysical group. After the event, one of the women asked me what the deeper meaning and point of evidential mediumship was. Was it really to prove survival of death? I shared with her that evidential mediumship may have started with proving life after death through evidence, but it really is all about healing. Mediumship is a powerful form of healing, as it can do for you what no other therapy can do in a matter of a few words. Knowing that their loved one is okay can bring peace to someone's heart. It can bring reassurance there is more to come after this life. It can also bring a sense of closure to situations that need a better ending and forgiveness.

The woman who attended the group reading didn't have a relation come through for her that day, and even though she thought it was interesting, she didn't understand why they brought through evidence that would seem mundane. For example, a mother who was obsessively ironing, a father who spent his retirement in his garden, or a brother who loved fishing. Also, why on Earth are they dredging up the past and some bringing apologies? Don't they have a life? Can't they move on?

I shared with her that, yes, of course, when our loved ones die, they go to the light, and there is also continuous existence of the afterlife. That even after their passing here on Earth, they will keep growing. Also, the things they choose to bring to the medium to talk about may seem mundane to the person not receiving a reading but could be incredibly memorable for the person receiving it. They never bring information through at random- there is meaning behind every piece of evidence. If the medium is skilled enough to go into the imagery, there is a whole story to be told about why they brought that piece of evidence through and what it really means on a deeper level. Mediumship has a way of retracting memories, talking about something they loved, or unfinished business. Sometimes, the information that comes through can be taken by maybe a few people (like a majority would have a grandmother who baked in the kitchen). Still, once you go a bit further with the information, it can unravel a whole story and be just for one person.

Also, the message is woven into the evidence, telling a story and purpose behind everything they choose to share. That is why your Great, Great, Great Grandmother doesn't come through for messages. They don't have a strong connection to you, nor would be able to bring you through any recognisable evidence because they move on with their existence on the other side. But your loved ones in spirit who you knew or are connected to your immediate/adopted family are watching over you. They continue to hang around and watch over you, and if they see you struggling or having discord in relationships or any area of your life, they will come through and offer you their love, support and forgiveness. They want to help you heal and evolve from where you are at so you can live your life fully, in expansion with continuous growth and evolvement in your life.

An example is when a woman comes to see me and is struggling in a relationship, and her dad was emotionally and/or physically abusive, and in spirit, he may come through to apologise for the things he did. Does that mean he's hanging around in spirit, waiting for those moments to say sorry? That is one way of looking at it, but another way of looking at it from a higher perspective is that your dad, in spirit, has gone to the light and with an eagle's view perspective, he can see things in a different light and how it affected his daughter. He may come through to offer forgiveness in order for his daughter to heal and have stronger relationships so that she can evolve, be self-empowered and feel better about herself moving forward. This scenario plays out quite frequently in spirit communication.

I think sometimes people think that our loved ones in spirit are just hanging around, or trying to clean things up and are haunting people. As humans we are the avatars, we are the ones in physical form having the human experience. When we are able to have openings, and free up energy to maximum capacity in this lifetime, things will continue our evolution on the other side, and that is why forgiveness is one of the highest forms of healing and can radically change your life. This is why Jesus preached forgiveness.

Another way to describe forgiveness is to unhook from the pain of the things that have happened to you and see things from another perspective where it's no longer weighing you down, having power over you so you can be free from it. When you can be free in this lifetime, the world is your oyster, and you can enjoy your time on Earth more instead of seeing it as a life sentence.

The Mother/Father Wound - Power Of Forgiveness

"Until we have seen someone's darkness. We don't really know who they are. Until we have forgiven someone's darkness, we don't really know what love is." - Marianne Williamson.

There has been a theme in my mediumship development circles that whenever a parent of one of my students crosses to spirit, they will continuously come through to get their message across until they have been heard. What I mean by this is if you choose to walk down the path of a medium, you will have to face your loved ones in spirit, whether you like it or not. I have led circles where a student comes to class all excited to learn mediumship but then ends up emailing me upset that every time she does partner work, her dad repeatedly comes through, and they had a rough relationship. And she wants to know why, even though she had already told him 'enough', did he keep returning?

When we walk the path as mediums, whatever is in our way blocking us will get revealed. As our sensitivity expands and heightens, the things that have held us back in life will start to be lifted and asked to be looked at. Usually, if you have unfinished business with a family member, they will take this great opportunity to come through and bring healing and closure. Now, of course, you are the medium and in control; if you are not ready, you can say so. But most likely, if your family member keeps trying to reach you, it's because it's time…

I have been studying spirituality for my whole adult life, and no matter what path I walk down or what spiritual practice I try to develop, healing of mother and father wounds is pivotal. To expand, you need to be able to face your family. It does not matter if they are alive or in spirit, or if you talk to them consciously or not. What is being asked of you is to be ready to face this. To find forgiveness in your heart not only for your family member but for yourself. It would be best to find compassion for that version of you that went through it.

Now I understand some family members are monsters, and I am not trying to paint people with a brush here. I know that true evil walks this world and that, for some of you, this is your family. But if you choose to develop your mediumship, hear them out if they come to you from spirit. Learning to create a new relationship with them today can be incredibly transformative. If they are in spirit, they are in a place where they have all the abilities to do that, all the support in the world, the evolution of their consciousness, and if they see you struggling or bypassing this and getting stuck, most likely they will come to you.

In my mediumship circles, I've seen transformed relationships. I had one circle member whose mother was a true narcissist and completely impossible to deal with. When she came to class, she would sigh as every student kept bringing through her mother in spirit.

"Again?!" She'd say, placing her hand over her forehead, wondering what the heck she had to say this time.

But as she grew as a person, a medium, and a healer, she gracefully developed a new relationship with her mother in spirit over the years. With laughter, as her mom comes through today, she can see that their relationship has been transformed by her being open to the spirit world and allowing herself to open up to their new relationship that can now evolve.

Death separates nothing. We are all connected in the web of life. To have these relationships with our family from the other side, as we grow and they evolve in spirit, is truly a gift. Finding peace, healing and humility for our family and their flaws can be humbling and awakening for you as you choose to see yourself within them. What you reject in your family lineage, you reject within you. You are not random in your family lineage. An elder in our community once told me that in order for a child to be born, our elders in spirit give consent for the child to be birthed into this world. You are not the special case that God got wrong. (Of course, I find this difficult to believe with rape survivors, but I hope on the other side I will get a deeper understanding of this).

At any point, you can choose to do better, make wiser choices for your life, and go beyond what they did and how they acted in their behaviour. But to see their humanity, what led to those selfish choices, disrespectful acts, or unforgettable pain they caused you, can set you free. In forgiveness, you are not saying what they did is okay. You are saying, *'I am no longer being a hostage of your abuse or letting it rule my life. I am free.'* When you are truly free, no emotion and no person can have power over you. You can see what we truly are: children of the creator, here to live an experience on Earth and do the best you can. You are choosing to lift the judgement of thinking life needs to play out any other way than it has for your growth and evolution.

Mediumship is truly life-changing. When you see yourself in your lineage, your family and your ancestors and see the gift of life you have inherited from them, you will live a life of appreciation and lightness. The baggage of the past will no longer hang over you. When this light has been ignited within you, you will help others to find this way to find freedom within their lives.

We are all one—all in the cosmic web of creation like a tapestry. Every act has a ripple effect. And when you choose love over darkness and open your heart to life, life will greet you, enrich you and give back to you. What you withhold from life, life withholds from you. So be free, lift those barriers, and choose to go beyond the walls and the blocks you have created. Look with compassion and love. There are no mistakes and no errors in this perfect order of the universe.

Lately, I have felt so liberated by the power of forgiveness that I will often check my inventory of my life to see if there is anyone I need to forgive from my past. Anyone I need to clean up discorded energy with. When I did my ministry training, I did this ruthlessly, taking accountability and making amends where it was needed. I have realised that any discord in my life is holding me back. Anywhere I can forgive or choose to see things differently will free up energy and open doors for me.

Can You Communicate With A Loved One Who's Reincarnated?

A woman named Sandy sat with me in a reading. She was asking about potential relationships with a man, and it seemed they never worked out, no matter how many relationships she had. She wanted to know what was wrong with her and what she needed to do to overcome this. As I closed my eyes and tuned in to deeply listen, I felt a tap on my right shoulder. A male presence moved close to me that felt like a father. I can't always explain how I know what I know, but I knew it was a strong presence who loved her dearly and watched over her. I told her I had a man here with me who showed up when she asked this question, and he felt like her dad. I asked her to validate yes or no. I asked her if she was open to receiving what he had to say, and she looked and seemed surprised he was there as it was not what she came for a reading for. She was specifically there for relationship guidance, not mediumship.

I shared that he enjoyed camping, fishing, and building fires but that his life got cut short, and it felt like something due to his heart. I felt this rush of energy in my chest all of a sudden, and I felt he died suddenly. I got a vision of him falling over. I shared how I saw visions of her as a little girl but not much beyond that. She started to cry as she recognised this to be her father. She told me he had been gone for 30 years. Why was he here? Why hadn't he reincarnated? To get over the death of her dad, she assumed that he would have done this by now, so she never bothered seeking out spirit communication with a medium as an adult. What was he doing looking out for her, especially regarding relationships? It was as if she was almost embarrassed that her dad was trying to help her with this from the other side. As if she had failed him.

He explained that he left when she was young but had never stopped being her father. He was aware of her struggles and what she was going through and wanted her to know he could help, but she needed to stop trying to figure everything out and let in help from the other side. She needed to ask him for help and find someone for her. She wiped her eyes with multiple tissues as tears streamed down her face, longing for that connection with the dad she had buried so long ago. Peace filled the room and replaced the figuring-it-out mind chatter she walked in with.

The opening that was witnessed in that session is something her dad, in spirit, knew she needed to stop trying to fill the void with the wrong men. She was worthy of loyalty, someone to look out for her, and her dad really was there and genuinely wanted to bring her someone if she let him. She needed to know she wasn't alone in this, and she needed to feel the love from her dad that was taken away and emptied so long ago. She felt the love from him fill the room.

After the reading, she asked me why he hadn't reincarnated. Why was he still there? He died so many years ago, she didn't understand why he was still watching over her, but at the same time, she was very grateful he showed up.

I explained to Sandy that when your loved one dies, if they were someone who was there for you in life, they will stay watching over you until it is your time to join them in spirit and beyond. They are not distracting you from something more significant. We are not pulling them down to Earth and waking the dead. They come to guide and show their love. Not to mention, I didn't go looking for a spirit to come to me. He came to me unannounced. I closed my eyes and got empty. The message came through when I stayed open to the experience.

The threads that join you between realms affect them in spirit just as much as it affects you. When you open your heart, you will free up energy that frees seven generations forward and seven generations back. This was a theory I was taught when I apprenticed with a shaman, and time and time again, as I witness miracles in a mediumship session, I see just how much is released and let go when contact is made between worlds (Earth and spirit) to bring messages through.

I also explained that her dad may be in spirit, but he is no longer confined to a physical body. He can actually be in multiple places at once. I demonstrate this in class when I have all my students tune into the same loved one in spirit. I have each of them bring through a piece of evidence about them (who they were, what they were like, an image, etc.), and each student is able to receive information all at the same time. I have demonstrated this in classes of up to 18 people. Each person has a unique experience with a spirit, all simultaneously happening at the same time. I reminded her that when we drop the physical body, we become one with all that is, something our minds cannot comprehend as humans. But our loved ones in spirit are only a thought away, yet they can be in multiple thoughts simultaneously.

This left me with a theory I believe to be true: that our loved ones in spirit can reincarnate and be in spirit all at the same time. That everything is happening everywhere all at once. There is no past or future, this is being proven by the world of Quantum Physics. The fractals in the universe are not limited to one body or one life, and your spirit cannot be contained. It is completely possible to have a physical life here on Earth while still feeling connected to all that is in the spiritual realms.

How To Connect To Your Ancestry

Part of your spiritual evolution as a human is acknowledging your ancestry and where you come from, to recognise your mother and father's lineage lines and to understand a deeper connection with those who watch over you.

Sometimes, when I give readings and bring through a loved one in spirit that the person only knew when they were a small child, like their grandmother or grandfather, they are surprised that they are there watching over them. They will say something like, *"But I barely knew them."* Even though you may not have had a tight relationship with a particular grandparent, it doesn't mean that that relationship ended when they died. If anything, they have become more interested in who you are and continue to watch over you from spirit.

It is taught in some shamanic traditions that when we heal ourselves it not only affects us, but seven generations back and seven generations forward. Our ancestors and family members watch over us. If you are a conscious being, being a family system pattern breaker (meaning you are willing to go beyond your family structure) and break family patterns like, for example, addiction, domestic violence or meanness, you will not only be doing it for yourself but your lineage as well.

Your family members in spirit will continue to watch over you to help you, guide you, and encourage you to go beyond the limited family structure that may have held them back in their lifetime. There will be times in your life you will catch yourself doing something and then realise that this has happened in your family before. For example, your mom gave to others to the point of exhaustion when you grew up, and she had serious health problems that stemmed from this. Now that you are an adult, you catch yourself over-giving yourself and developing serious health conditions similar to your mother.

It can be frustrating and comforting to know that you were not the first in your family to experience this, but having the awareness means you are being called to break this cycle. To do what maybe your mother couldn't do and now make positive changes in your life to change the patterning. To take your power back and set boundaries, be there for yourself and ask for help where needed. Whatever feels true to you in the situation.

Sometimes while giving a reading, I'll hear about how my client is unhappy in her marriage. It may come up that her mother was unhappy in her marriage, and her grandmother too. I remember one reading I gave where I saw this woman's grandmother look like a cheerleader as she was cheering her on from spirit as this woman empowered herself by stepping out of the marriage. Something her grandmother wasn't able to do in her lifetime, but wished she could.

Choosing to acknowledge your lineage can be incredibly healing for you, as well as a way to not feel so isolated in your struggles. It's also a way to reconnect to the gifts of your family lines and take on their positive attributes instead of just remembering their negative ones. Each one of us has four family lineages (mom's mom and dad's lines, as well as dad's mom and dad's lines) that we can make a connection to.

Just because you don't have a personal relationship with them in person, or only had a short relationship with them when you were young, does not stop you from connecting with them in spirit.

Here are some steps on how to create this:

· Create and build an altar separate from other altars around your home.

· Place a cloth over the table. (The colour of the cloth is personal to you. I prefer red as it symbolises power, or white as it's clean and fresh, symbolising renewal.)

· Place a new candle in the middle of the altar. I prefer a white candle as it symbolises the white light, but use what you have or are drawn to. There is no wrong way of doing this if you have good intentions.

· Place photographs of your mother and father on each side of the candle. I like to put mom on the left side to symbolise the feminine and father on the right side to symbolise the masculine.

· Place photographs of your grandmothers and grandfathers on each side accordingly- behind your mom's and your dad's sides. If you do not have access to photos of each of them, you can place a belonging or a piece of paper with their names on it. You can put "grandma, grandpa" on the paper if you do not know their names. (Call them what you would have - Oma, Nana, etc.) Be creative and use what you have. Just that acknowledgement allows you room to grow your evolving relationship.

· If you knew your great-grandparents or great-great-grandparents, place them on your altar in the correct order behind your grandparents.

· Light the candle when you are home and want to acknowledge their presence. Say an intentional prayer out loud to symbolise what this means. For example: "*I light this candle in honour of my family lineage. I ask to deepen my relationship with my family members.*" Keep the prayer simple and intentional.

This can be nice to do in your evenings when you are home from work or on your days off. As you light the candle, take time to acknowledge each of your loved ones and even speak aloud a question you may have for them.

Sometimes, working with one family member at a time is nice. You may place their photo upfront or lay something over a photograph of something that was theirs. You may place fresh flowers on your altar to acknowledge them or a specific loved one/ancestor.

Please notice what happens over time by having an altar set up to acknowledge their presence. Remember, when an altar is set up, it is there to "alter your thoughts", so treat it respectfully and sacredly. Avoid placing coffee cups, books, kids' toys, etc. on the altar. Please keep it clean and intentional for what it is there for.

You may notice an idea pop into your mind, a place you want to visit, or intense dreams. I know for myself when I did this, all of a sudden, I had a huge desire to learn French. (My grandparents on my mom's side were French). I honoured this by buying the DuoLingo App on my phone and learning French. I also had an urge to see my grandfather's cabin, which he built a few hours from me. I drove to see it, realising I was looking at the property with new eyes. I also went to my grandmother's gravesite and brought flowers. These were simple ways I honoured my grandparents. I didn't have an understanding of this when I was a younger person when they passed away. It's the inspired action you take to help you reconnect with your family.

You will notice that the more you take time to acknowledge them and get to know them in spirit form, the more compassion you will develop for your family lineage. This will open and awaken you to new possibilities that may have not been awakened before. It will also help you realise your likeness or what qualities you have of theirs. Do not let the fact that they are no longer here physically block you from getting to know them and having a personal relationship with you. They are a part of you. They want to know you.

For those of you who have grandparents or other family members you do not respect or are disgusted with, do not rush to do this exercise. Invite those on your altar who feel good to you and are ready for you to get to know them first. Over time, you may feel an urge to get to know a grandparent or great-grandparent in another way if they did acts or behaviours you do not respect or approve of. But take your time. When you set up an altar, you are asking to go beyond the physical limitations of the body to the higher self. Understand that even those who committed harmful acts here on Earth are in spirit, a place of pure love. You may long to understand them more, as they will also want to share with you.

Also, know that you are not here to carry their wounds for them but to shed light and go beyond. Let this be an intimate journey with them. You are not here to do their work for them but to release and let go of the burdens you may carry that are no longer needed. Let this be a freeing experience. Know that what you judge in your ancestry, you have not accepted within yourself. We are all capable of harmful acts, although you may have decided for yourself to do better. You are the next generation moving beyond what they were capable of. Let yourself know them, hear them and move forward with greater love and compassion for them and yourself.

In 2018, I was driving to the Spiritualist Centre I am now the minister of and all of a sudden, I started to think about my grandfather's brother on my mother's side, my great uncle. Just the thought of him made me shudder. He was a man who was always around when I was little, and he was a mason (interesting at that time that the Spiritualist Church was located in a mason's hall). He was a businessman who I felt used to trick people to get ahead. He used to ask me to babysit his dog while he went to the Masonic hall and say he would pay me, then conveniently forget his money. I didn't like him. I despised him so much that I forgot his existence and moved on until that day.

I was driving to the Spiritualist Centre, and he popped into my awareness. Because I had done this altar exercise before, I took the time to recognise his oversoul instead of blocking him out of my consciousness. I welcomed his higher self-presence. I looked at the qualities I did have of his. I was a business owner, I was a part of a centre that was a Mason's hall, yet I was a spiritualist. I loved dogs, and I even loved his dog. I also enjoyed travelling around the world like he did. All these qualities that he had, I had too. He just made some poor decisions in his free will that tainted him from my view. But I felt compassion instead of rejection for the first time.

When I got to the centre that day, I sat quietly in the audience, only to have him come through with his little dog in spirit to apologise for his selfish acts. He even mentioned how he scammed me as a kid out of money! (I was seven at the time.) After that day, he never came through again (to date), but I found peace in him being there and coming through. The medium had to shake him off afterwards, saying, *"Yuck!"* I laughed. I knew exactly what she was talking about. But then we laughed, realising that once it's done, everyone, not only me but our whole ancestry, will receive the ripple effect.

You feel complete when you feel a sense of completion with your altar, meaning you no longer feel such an urge to spend time with it. Dismantle the altar. Thank your family members for being there with you and keeping that relationship evolving. It does not have to end if they are not with you on the altar. When needed, feel free to set it up again. You can do this with children who have passed, getting to know them now as they grow with you on the other side. You could do this with friendships too. All our relationships are spiritual. Each person has a meaning for being in our lives, and it can be a great blessing to continue your relationship with them and understand their new evolved self from the non-physical world.

Evolution Of The Soul

"My goal is not to be better than anyone else, but to be better than I used to be." - Wayne Dyer

When our loved one dies, do they automatically get enlightened?

This is a question I have sat with quite a bit. What happens when our loved ones in spirit die? Do they become fully realised? Do they get blinded by the light and suddenly see a bird's eye view of their life and want to immediately start cleaning things up to make it easier for their loved ones in spirit left behind? I feel this answer is a paradox as it's a yes and a no.

Quite often, as I have shared, when a loved one dies, and they had hang-ups in life or were unkind, it's common that they will come through in a reading and apologise. They will see how they affected their loved ones and want to help them so they can live their best life. They will see how their actions have affected the ones left behind and want to clear any rifts. I see this, more often than not, being a huge part of the work I do.

But every now and then, it isn't like that. I can think of a couple of situations in particular where this was not the case.

When a loved one dies, they experience a continuous evolution of the soul, meaning that they cannot die, and they will continue growing on the other side. There is no limit to their expansion, and they will continue to evolve. It is taught by many new age beliefs that to come to Earth is a great opportunity, the fast track for souls' growth. Many souls come here to grow rapidly for their continuous existence on the other side. Just like on Earth, we have roles or jobs we tend to. On the other side, it is believed that we continue our service in a way that resonates with us for our highest good. Often, someone who is a healer in life will continue being a healing force from the other side. Or someone who helped many will continue to help family, even when they are crossed over. It is in our nature to want to serve and give, and in our souls' evolution that continues wherever we go, it's part of who we are.

But every now and then, I will be placed in a reading where I see a person sitting in front of me waiting to hear from their person. I can't call them loved ones, but maybe ex-husband, baby daddy, or sex offender family member, and they will be waiting for the big apology. But the apology doesn't come.

How they come through in spirit will be similar to who they were. They may still carry that wall of energy or lack of self-expression they could never give you. They will show me as the medium the relationship and how they are bonded.

I had this man come through in spirit for my client Cindy. He showed me he was creating distance with her and had a big, bravado-type presence. He shared that he thought he was great, puffed himself up and made himself look really important. By the way she was acting, I could tell this man had caused her a lot of pain and suffering. Her hands were wrapped around her waist. She looked down, and her face was red with tears.

She kept saying to me, *"Is there something he wants to say to me?"*

I would tune back into him. He continued sharing about the car he drove and what he was good at in life, and the deeper I tried to pull him in, the more distance I felt was created.

I shared with her that, even though I knew she was waiting for something (an apology), I didn't feel he was directing the reading that way. If anything, I felt he wanted to continue talking about his life and where he was. He shared from spirit that he knew she wanted him to come that day in the reading, and if she had something to say, she should say it, but he had nothing to say to her.

At this point in the reading, I felt more like a mediator. I wasn't sure what was happening, but I did my best to stay out of the way and be the medium- the messenger between worlds. She told me she was disappointed. She was waiting for him to say he was sorry for what he had done and that he would help their son. But he didn't. She shared with me that her son had not been doing well at all mentally, and that she had many cursing matches at him in spirit about why he wasn't doing something about it and letting their son get so mentally ill.

I understood her frustration for not getting the answers she hoped for, but she said it also made sense why he hadn't helped. He still wasn't there yet. She told him that he could not be a part of their son's life until he got his life together and grew up. Unfortunately, he took that to heart, as this was still not the case, even on the other side.

We joked that he must have been a young spirit, new to this evolution thing. Who knows what the future could hold? But at this moment, he was not the spirit to pray for help from. Many other loved ones in spirit were willing and ready to step in and take it from there. They came first in the reading and kept saying they wanted to help. Only at the end of the reading could she see what that meant: that they were all willing to step in instead.

I had this woman come to see me, and from the moment she sat down, she said she had been waiting for this reading for a long time and was so excited it was that day. I started the reading, opened myself up, and felt the presence of a father standing with me. I shared this with her and noticed that I thought he was quite confrontational as he drew close. All the hairs on my neck rose as I felt I needed to walk on eggshells when dad was around. She understood the information and said, *"Yes,"* with a smirk. *"and...."*

I shared a bit about his life, his upbringing, his alcoholism, and his anger. She understood all of it. I talked about their distant relationship and the fact he was never there. She understood.

"And..." she said again, waiting for something.

Psychically, I knew she was waiting for the big apology, the *"You were right"*, but the more I connected to him, the less I felt it was going that way. He was sharing his story and his perspective, what it was like to be him, and why he was the way he was. The mediumship did not lead to a great apology. If anything, it was showing the opposite - that he needed forgiveness.

I shared this with her. I said, *"Your dad is here. He is telling his story, but I feel a lot of judgement from you to him of the way he was."* I looked at her and said, *"Trust me, I can understand why."* She laughed. *"But he is asking you to listen. He says he needs you to understand him, and the apology works both ways. Unfortunately, he is not saying he is sorry. He wants you to open your heart a bit more to him."*

Her face looked shocked. She tapped her foot on the floor and looked enraged. I saw her face go red and her fists clenched. *"This was not what I was expecting,"* she said, pissed off.

I stayed calm and made eye contact with her as I nodded. My job as a medium is to bring that reunion between two worlds but to stay with the spirit and not get sucked into the client and say whatever I feel she wants me to say. My duty as a medium is to represent the spirit word.

I felt her dad stand firm with me. He was hurt, but his armour was off. I could tell who he was, but I could also tell that her need for forgiveness wouldn't add to her healing. She, too, had to open her heart to her father, and until that happened, nothing would change. I trusted what was going on here. I trusted the intelligence of spirit. I understand now more than ever that our loved ones in spirit come through to forgive as an opportunity for growth for their loved ones here, but it's not a band-aid solution to helping people's minds know they are right, that they played no part in the relationship.

The reading closed, and she was not happy. She said she knew I was doing my job and that I did the best I could. I had brought him through. She hoped he would have been different now that he could see what he had put her through as his daughter. I understood. I consoled and reminded her of what her dad said, that it takes two to open our hearts, that when she was ready to drop her judgements and pains of him, then it would happen. I encouraged her to go through her anger, to really let herself go there. Often, in readings, it's when we get angry that the reading doesn't always progress. Anger is a huge part of feeling emotions; we must find ways to express it healthily. When we do that, the energy can move and free up space for love, and that is what was needed for this healing to occur.

It's the same in life when we are mad at someone and won't forgive them until they forgive us. We could be waiting our whole lifetime or lifetimes. When you choose your happiness over righteousness, you can be free today. That freed-up space can create openings that were never there before. Forgiveness is not about someone else giving you what you want so you can be happy; you must make peace with yourself first, and when that occurs, miracles can happen.

Even though I believe that when we pass away, we are embraced and expanded by the light, I also believe that, just like here on Earth, we are all at different levels of our evolution in consciousness. Maybe that's why it's such a draw to come here.

Hul'q'umi'num Language

First Nations Cowichan elder Lana Ryan gave full permission for this book to include information about the native language and some cultural traditions in the Cowichan Valley for teaching purposes.

I was asked to do a celebration of life for my good friend Lana's mother. Her mother was a First Nations elder in our community in Cowichan Valley. Speakers came up to honour her mother, and one of the elders, also her nephew, spoke a few words.

In Hul'q'umi'num language (the native language spoken on Vancouver Island, Canada from Malahat to Nanoose Bay) it is asked to refer to your loved one in spirit as they are in spirit, to no longer refer to them as mom or dad in present tense, but to refer to them as 'mom in spirit'. This allows room for the relationship to evolve into what it is now and acknowledge the lineage. It allows the relationship to evolve into what it is today, a continuing relationship with where they are now.

In the Hul'q'umi'num language, referring to your parents in spirit would be pronounced *mom tenulth* or *dad menulth*.

It is important to continue your relationship with your mom, dad, brother and sister, even when they pass away from the physical realm, to continue to honour them in spirit. This keeps the relationship alive and evolving in the continuous existence in the afterlife. They may be deceased in physical form, but they are not dead. Their spirit is more active than ever, and nothing can separate you. It takes time to adjust to the relationship with them in spirit, but by keeping them included in your life they can show you how they are still with you. They may come as a sign through nature, birds, animals, synchronicity and people etc..

I am so grateful to live in the Cowichan Valley on Vancouver Island and to be able to learn from the elders. There is nothing unnatural about communing with your ancestors, it is a part of life, and so it should be. Having the privilege to learn from First Nations culture by living in the valley has softened my heart and has humbled me to see the world differently. Communication with the afterlife is far from new age but goes back to the beginning of time.

A client shared with me that over the years of getting used to her parents no longer being with her, she has allowed herself to see her parents in all of life and creation. When she sits at the beach in the morning to say her prayers and the seal swims by, she says, "*Thanks, dad in spirit*". When the hummingbird comes to her bird feeder in the evenings as she has dinner, she says, "*Hi mom in spirit*". These are ways she keeps that door open and gives the invitation for even more connection.

You may ask, *but how do I know I am not making this up*? Just remember, your loved one who died has returned to all of creation, to all that is, to oneness. They are now a part of you and cannot be separated. If you choose to see them as gone, dead and unable to communicate, you will create more of that. But if you choose to see them in all of life, a collective web, they will join you in all that you do and bless you with miracles every day through connection.

Chapter 11:
Transformation

~

Ministry

"No matter what despair, no matter what misfortune, you stand there with love still radiating from you. Then God will touch you. You will have been chosen then as a channel for the Great Spirit."

- Gordon Higginson from *Finding The Spirit Within* (audio extract from lecture)

In January 2018 I was invited to Nanaimo by Reverend Malcolm Gloster to visit Two Worlds Spiritualist Centre. At the time it was a spiritualist centre I hadn't been to. I had only attended services at Cowichan Valley Spiritualist Church of Healing and Light. I was getting more involved there and invited to chair services in Cowichan, and I was even blessed enough to start doing one or two mediumship messages during the mediumship part of the service with whoever was the medium that day, even though I was chairing.

Malcolm wanted me to see more churches on this island, so he picked me up and we drove to Nanaimo together. It was such a different centre with such a unique feel. I was warmly greeted, and there were a few familiar faces, so I felt immediately welcome.

Malcolm introduced me to Elizabeth, the president at the time, and told her he'd like to invite me to do a service with him in the future and was wondering if they would allow it. They loved that idea, and I was placed on the roster quite quickly. Two Worlds was always open to new ideas, guest mediums and ways to build community.

Malcolm and I drove up again and we did a double service. The thing about Malcolm and I working together is that we usually get hit with the giggles. In our mediumship demonstration, we would bring heartfelt and humourous connections from spirit and our connection was always in flow and harmony when we worked together.

After this service, I was invited to do another one, but this time with Reverend Dianne Burrough. They were celebrating their 10th anniversary of Two Worlds, and they thought it would be great to have more mediums working, so they invited Dianne and I to join together for this special service. I had known Dianne because she was a minister in the community, and her warm heart and grace always drew me towards her. She married Matthew and I in 2016 and also became a friend of mine just from being around Spiritualism. She and I are kindred spirits, and without even having to get to know each other well, we knew each other immediately from a soul level.

That day at the 10th-anniversary event, they announced a surprise during the service- that Dianne would become the new minister at the centre. Paul Bishop, who previously ran the place as the head medium, had retired and also passed away quite quickly afterwards in 2017. Unfortunately, I did not get the chance to know him, and the centre felt called to continue running, even though he was no longer with us, but they really needed a new minister. Dianne had run her own spiritualist church in Nanoose Bay for two years, but for various reasons, she had to close it.

That day, Dianne announced that she would be the new minister of Two Worlds. As it was being announced, this whoosh of energy moved through me from behind. I had head-to-toe goosebumps, my eyes started leaking and I was looking for a tissue to wipe my face. Everyone stood up and clapped when they heard Dianne would become the new minister. There were close to one hundred people there that day. As I gathered my excitement that Dianne would be taking over, the energy that moved through me quickly spoke to me in a male voice through my soul, "*You're next*".

That day, as I drove home, I noticed that when I got in the car, I felt the presence of Paul Bishop sitting next to me. He winked at me and said, "*We've got big plans for you,*" and then continued to sit with me the car ride home, warming me up to the idea of being a part of Two Worlds.

The feeling stayed with me and it wouldn't go away. About one week later, I wrote Dianne a Facebook message and told her I was so excited to hear she would be the minister of Two Worlds and that some interesting things were happening to me since that service. It was like something pushed me to write her. I didn't want to tell anyone, but I couldn't hide it. It was getting louder by the day, and I couldn't make the feeling stop or go away.

Dianne replied, *"Nicole, if you are being called to ministry, you should let me know."*

I didn't respond for a while, maybe a few days. As far as I knew, you didn't get to choose to be a minister on this island where we lived, but the spirit world and the minister chose. I didn't want to interfere with the process, but after a few days of not writing back to Dianne, I felt strongly about writing to her. *"I feel we should talk about this."* I included some things about Paul Bishop and him coming into my car in spirit.

Dianne invited me to see her at her house for a meeting. A few weeks later, I drove two hours to her house. *"What was happening?"* I thought. *"How was I to become a minister when I had no religion growing up in my home?"* I thought. But I let it go and thought I would let it unfold naturally if it were meant to be.

When I got to Dianne's house, she sat me down and decided to fill me in on what it entailed to become a minister- the apprenticeship process, the mentoring, the assignments, learning to do complete services myself, weddings, funerals, and joining the board of directors. It was a lot to take in. Of course, the feeling and the calling came from within, and hearing all these things sounded like a lot to take on, but not necessarily like something I could do on an already full-time workload and living my life. Not to mention that this was a volunteer position. No minister is paid a salary to live and be a minister.

Dianne also warned me that the mentorship process was a lot, and it was more than the actual book work, but an internal process I'd have to go through.

Dianne laid it out to me straight that day. But that if I was called, I was called, and I would have to accept it. Even if I fought it all the way through.

As I left her house that day, I walked through her parking lot with my head held low. I had no idea what to do. This felt like way too much. How could I be taking on more? Well, I couldn't. I would have to eliminate things to make room. I also felt that maybe I wasn't truly being called, but I got an idea and was running with it. What if it was my ego? Or was I getting in my own way?

As I clicked my beeper on my car to unlock it, I looked up at the sky and said, *"Pioneers of Spiritualism, I call on you now. This is just too big for me. I need your help. If I am meant to do this, if you support my decision to represent spiritualism, I ask that you give me an undeniable sign. Very obvious. Because I cannot and will not do this without your permission and full guidance to represent spiritualism. This is far too big for me."*

I got in my car and started driving in silence. I needed to process what was being said. As I turned on the side streets to get onto the highway, I turned left. The car I let pass me before turning onto the road stood out. The license plate said *"GORDON"*. Gordon was the name of one of the finest mediums of our time. Gordon was my Spiritualist idol, whom I looked up to in spiritualism as a medium, minister, former president of the SNU (Spiritualist National Union) and pioneer. He passed away in 1993, but many follow his legacy and continue his teachings. He has his picture on the wall of the Arthur Findlay College. He wrote an amazing book *"On The Side Of Angels"* about his lifetime of service as a medium.

For the whole two-hour car ride home, I followed this car in front of me. The whole time! As I drove, I felt his presence and Gordon say to me, *"I will be with you on this journey, the whole way. This is my promise that I will never leave you."*

As I turned off the highway to my house, I saw the car drive away. It was so powerful and so meaningful. I didn't waste any time. I wrote to Dianne immediately and told her what happened. She replied, *"Alright then, Nicole, let's begin."*

January 2021

Three years later, almost to the day, I was getting ready for my exams. I was feeling immense doubt. My health deteriorated; I hadn't slept in 3 years, I was still managing some health problems I had faced over the last year and was exhausted. I was so done I wasn't sure if I wanted to do this anymore.

I was driving to Duncan after talking with Dianne about setting dates for my exam. As I went to Duncan, I said, *"Spirit and Pioneers of Spiritualism, if you still want me to do this, please show me an undeniable sign."* Within a minute of saying this, I turned the bend on the road and there in front of me was the exact car I had seen three years earlier with the license plate *"GORDON"*. I felt his presence, and then he said, *"I promised I would never leave you."*

I smiled and a power within me instantly filled me up and recharged me. I got this, I am ready....

Coming Full Circle

"Empowerment is realising you are the one who needs to say the things you've waited your entire life to hear."- Matt Kahn.

May 2018

Reverend Dianne Burrough asked me to be her student minister, but it came with a health warning. She wished this was something she didn't need to bring up with me, but she cared about me too much, not to mention it. She had witnessed most mediums, if not all, had dealt with a health crisis upon their training into becoming Spiritualist Ministers. For what she had witnessed, including her own training, it was tumultuous.

I thought about it. The calling was stronger than what I was hearing. Not to mention, I felt I already had my health crisis awakening, where I had a near-death to propel me on this path. *"Maybe I could skip over that part again?"* I thought. *"Maybe I could reclaim my power from that creation?"* I didn't feel I needed to go through that again. Not in my training anyway.

May 2020

The global pandemic was two months in, and stress surrounded me. I had completely converted my business from doing readings and running circles to online. Our spiritualist centre was finding ways we could still offer services: writing, audio, and keeping in touch through newsletters. It was a quick, dramatic shift, and as much as it was going well, the stress of the unknown was completely gut-wrenching. How long was it going to be like this? Could I handle being a medium and student minister during this time when it seemed like the lives of every person I talked to had been tipped upside-down? Opinions, chaos, and conspiracies were starting, and it felt like it went from *"We are all in this together"* to *"What side are you on with vaccines?"*

I was struggling and trying to keep it together. I was dealing with migraines almost daily, waiting for an MRI later that month to have a brain scan, as daily migraines for six months are not normal. I had been doing the ketogenic diet for about a year at this point, and I had lost 40 pounds. Everyone kept telling me how great I looked, but my body started responding differently. I was starting to have stomach pain. At first, I ignored it, thinking I just needed to take some extra digestive enzymes or remember to take my probiotic in the morning. But late at night, I started having these attacks. It reminded me and gave me flashbacks to when I was dealing with my appendix pain 12 years earlier. I used to panic about stomach pain, but nothing that couldn't be easily resolved with probiotics, digestive enzymes or liquorice root, so I tried to brush this off as that.

At 11 pm one night, the pain came on quickly. I was buckled over on the floor—on my hands and knees and moaning. I thought I was going to die as my insides felt like they were being wrenched, and no position, no thought process, no extra strength Ibuprofen was going to resolve it. I tried to lay in bed, pacing around the house and ignoring it, but it felt like the more I tried to do, the worse it got.

Matthew was aware of my tendencies to be maybe a bit dramatic when it comes to stomach stuff and thought perhaps he'd call the nurse's line. We were in the pandemic and told to stay away from the emergency department unless it really was an emergency. The nurse on the line could hear me moaning and groaning, asking me on a scale of 1 to 10 how bad the pain was. Staring into the phone, laying on the ground on speaker, I said, *"9.5. If it were a 10, I'd be passed out."* She told me to call 911 and to get an ambulance. But being a little shy and maybe a bit proud, there was no way I'd let an ambulance with sirens come to our house, as I didn't want the whole neighbourhood wondering what was going on at our house at midnight. So, I convinced Matthew to drive me 20 minutes to the local small-town hospital in Duncan.

He dropped me off at the curb, as he was not allowed into the emergency department. I slogged in, having flashbacks of my 22-year-old self walking into the emergency department with my hand over my stomach. Here I was, repeating a similar pattern I had lived before. A year of obsessive dieting, stomach pain I couldn't resolve on my own, being dropped off at the curb of the emergency, and walking into the hospital. I was ready for a battle and a fight as I didn't want to be told it was nothing and brushed off. That scenario many moons ago taught me I needed to be assertive and ask for my needs. I wasn't going to be quiet. I was going to be clear, tell them what was going on, the symptoms, and what I needed.

I approached the administration, grabbing one of those disposable masks as I sat at the counter with the glass between us. I looked her straight in the eye and told her, *"I need help. I am having stomach pain. A 9.5 out of 10 kind of pain. I have been here before, and I have done this before. I am one of those people who don't look like they are in pain when they really are. I am telling you this because I really need your help."*

I then asked her for a bucket as I bent over and vomited. With it being COVID times, of course, anything flying out of my mouth was considered an enormous risk, and the receptionist behind the glass started typing things in fast as I slapped my care card on the desk. She heard me and, without wasting time, sent me directly into the back and had me lay down in one of the hospital beds.

There I was, staring back up at the neon lights above me like I had 12 years ago. I was teary thinking about it. I was in excruciating pain, unable to sit still, and I had no idea how long I was going to be back there in this brick-enclosed room by myself. I was in a sterile environment alone without a nurse or doctor in sight in the middle of the night on a weekday.

'Patterns repeat themselves' I thought to myself as I lay there, afraid for my life. Maybe that was initiation #1, 12 years ago, but now I seemed to be experiencing initiation #2. I had no idea what was going on or why I needed to go through something like this again. Like I said, I was hypervigilant regarding my stomach health. I had had blood tests and ultrasounds before in the past few years, all indicating I was healthy. It was my migraines that were my major issue. I thought my stomach issues were in the past.

I rolled over onto my side and sent a message via WhatsApp to my friend Jason Goldsworthy in Germany. It was 9 hours ahead, so it felt safe to message, knowing it was daytime for him. He was my medium friend, a nurse and a great healer. I asked him if he could send me spiritual healing, that I was in the emergency ward and needed to ask a favour. He answered immediately, saying yes to the request, and started sending me distance trance healing from where he was in that moment. Probably the breakfast table.

I instantly relaxed as I felt myself beginning to be wrapped in white light. My breathing softened, and the pain started to decrease immediately. Healing energy always worked for me, and I drifted off to sleep and became still as the healing was sent to me. I felt hugely comforted at that moment.

The nurse walked in, taking my blood pressure and asking me questions, but I stayed relatively quiet. When the doctor walked in, he saw me calmly lying there and asked me what was going on. It was a different person who walked in there half an hour ago, puking at the administration desk, demanding to skip the line and put me straight through with my 9.5 pain. Even though the pain was decreasing immensely because of the healing being currently sent my way, intelligence came over me that this was my chance to get the help I needed if I spoke up.

I told him about my sudden pain at 11 pm, the buttercream icing cake I had indulged in earlier, that it was stabbing on my upper right side, and I had a full abdomen. I told him about my appendix and that it was the same pain I had had 12 years ago (cutting feeling), and I wasn't leaving until he did blood work, an ultrasound and an X-ray on me. I knew it was COVID time, and I wouldn't have come here unless it was an emergency.

He examined my stomach, asking whether my right shoulder and back hurt, and I said no. He asked me if it came on gradually or intensely, and I let him know intensely and fast. He asked me if I had been burping or had a history of indigestion. He let me know it was the middle of the night, so no X-rays or ultrasounds could be done as they didn't have midnight staff for that, but he was going to give me a pink lady to calm my digestive tract. Also, he could provide me with something for the pain, but he couldn't do anything more for me at that moment.

Thinking to myself, *why do I even bother?* The spiritual healing was doing more for me than this guy. But I was also being respectful of his medical checklist process. I agreed to the morphine injection, in case the pain came back suddenly when I left the building and a pink lady drink that was supposed to calm my digestive tract.

I knew something was seriously wrong; this could go on for weeks, and I knew I was smarter and wiser than I used to be. He could not help me with what I was asking for unless I was transparent, honest and communicative. I told him I needed to return for an ultrasound and an X-ray when the department opened in the morning. He said okay and wrote it on his chart. I assured him again that I wouldn't be here unless it were severe. He smiled and agreed, offering me kindness, which I needed. He had a crash cart where he did a mini ultrasound on my stomach, and as he did it, he didn't find anything.

"It could be indigestion," he said. *"You should be better in a few days; it will work itself out."* Those words shot through my mind. 'Geesh,' I thought, 'who's writing the script?' Why does it always have to be word for word when you are reliving a traumatic experience?

"Okay. I'll see you in the morning."

I left the emergency department. Matthew had stayed waiting in the parking lot for me. It was now 2:30 am, and he was talking to his mother in England on WhatsApp, trying to stay awake so he could drive us home when I got out. He had no idea how long I was going to be in there. And to be honest, I wasn't sure if he was even still there. I was in my own world, and it was hard to think about anyone or anything else but the paint I was in. The morphine made me feel comfortably numb. We drove home in silence, and I slept like a log for the rest of the night.

I kept my phone close to me, waiting for the hospital to phone any moment and call me back in for that emergency ultrasound. They didn't.

The whole day went by, and I was scared to eat. I didn't want to disrupt my gut, and I didn't want to have another attack of whatever the heck that was. So, I laid low and slept most of the day, chewing Ibuprofen every 6 hours. The next day rolled around, and the phone rang around noon. It was the emergency department. They were ready to have me back for that ultrasound. I grabbed my coat and ran out the door. I was there within half an hour.

After the ultrasound, I started putting on my shoes and grabbing my purse, knowing well that the ultrasound tech wasn't allowed to say anything to me. She casually said, "*So, who can I contact to give them the information to ensure you get a follow-up.*"

"*The doctor that was in emergency that night? I don't know...Oh wait, call my GP. She's on it with these things.*"

And I walked out the door.

When I got home half an hour later, my phone rang, and it was my doctor's office. My doctor was calling.

"Nicole?" She asked me, concerned. *"How are you doing?"*

"Oh, I am okay, just a bit under the weather", I replied.

"What are you doing right now?"

"Nothing; I guess I was waiting for someone to call," I told her. My doctor had been someone I had grown to love and trust over the years. She seemed to understand my hypervigilant requests for my health and always went above and beyond for me.

"So, I looked at your charts and your ultrasound. You have a gallbladder that's full of stones. It also looks like your gallbladder is inflamed acutely, and you are going to need surgery. Can you go to Victoria?"

"Huh?" I said, as my eyes grew as wide as saucers. *"Now?! Aren't we in the pandemic? Am I even allowed to have this right now?"* I was thinking of the news and social media where they made people feel complete guilt or shame for needing hospital care. Showing pictures of people dying of heart attacks at home as they were not allowed in hospitals. Then I thought, yeah, that probably was quite dramatic, and it is not a good idea to believe everything you read or see on TV or Facebook.

"Nicole, you do not want another attack. This is painful, and it's serious. It would be best if you didn't put this off much longer. Also, with the state of COVID, I don't know when you will have another chance. If I call in a scheduled surgery, you could be waiting months. I don't want this for you."

I took a deep breath. Surgery, holy smokes. I think about the nine months that followed my surgery for my appendix and all the surgical trauma that came with that. *"Can't I heal this on my own?"* I said, thinking about stone flushes and such. Then, I remembered I was talking to a GP, not my naturopath.

"Uh, Nicole, not when it's acute like this."

"Okay, fine. I will do this." I said as I calmed myself down and committed to following through on her requests for me.

"I will call the emergency department now at Vic General. Have them add you to the roaster, and wait at home until I call you back about when to leave. Once I know the wait, you can go down there."

I hung up the phone, appreciating at that moment how much I loved her thoroughness. She truly was the best and always there for me. I cleared my calendar, packed an overnight bag and waited for my call. I couldn't help but wonder what the heck I had just committed to and if this was actually a good idea.

She called back 2 hours later. *"6 am. I need you there bright and early. They will do an intake and then start preparing you for surgery. Don't eat anything before then."*

"Okay," I replied, trusting her but feeling frightened by this rational life-changing decision without contacting my naturopath first. But the wave came over me, and she said the word "acute." I knew there wasn't a way back from this once I got to this point. Thinking about the pain the night before, I cringed. *"Nope,"* I said to myself. *"I may be all love and light and eat healthy, but I cannot do that again."*

The morning couldn't come fast enough. I was hungry and thirsty, and I had this gnawing pain in my gut. I felt lightheaded and concerned I would get a migraine for the disruption I was going through. I was second-guessing if taking the surgery was a rational decision. Maybe if I shared it with friends, they would think I was jumping the gun. Usually, I was always willing to try a remedy first or at least consult a second opinion. But I was thrown right into this. I was fearing what my life would be like, with not only a missing appendix but a missing gallbladder, too. What was my digestion going to be like then? I would have to stop eating keto. My eyes widened, thinking about the weight I may gain back if I started eating carbs again. This year, I had slimmed down, and the last thing I wanted was to gain my quarantine 15. Yikes.

As I lay in bed, waiting for my turn, I started to pray. *"Oh God, please help me. Even though I am lying in the hallway in a hospital bed, can you please give me a sign that my guide or an angel is with me?"* I need to know this was the right decision.

Within minutes, a woman in scrubs, glasses and a medical mask approached me and placed her hands on the side of the bed.

"Nicole Powell?" She said to me.

I turned my head, and with all the gear she had on, I could not recognise her face.

"Nicole, you gave me a reading," she said back to me with the sincerest look on her face.

"Oh my God!" I shouted as my eyes filled up with tears. *"I was just laying here praying for God to send me an angel and let me know I am going to be okay, and here you are. My Earth angel."*

I could see her smiling with her eyes. She was there to protect me. *"Nicole, you are going to be just fine. You have the top anesthesiologist today, an amazing surgeon. I will be with you the whole time. Trust me, you will be well looked after."*

A huge weight just fell off of me. I was okay. Everything was okay. I made the right decision. I could let go now. I didn't need to second guess myself. I knew without a doubt I was led to this moment that I would be alright. I felt the warmth of spirit all around me. My eyes wept with tears, knowing that I could be of service to her and now she was here helping me. She truly is the most gifted nurse anyone could ask for. She is kind, considerate, caring, educated and good at her job.

I was carted into the room for surgery and prepped to be put under. I couldn't stop myself from thinking in my head, *"Oh God, please don't let me die, not today. Send all your healers, angels and healing guides around me for this surgery"*.

As she placed the mask over my face and asked me to start taking some deep breaths, my whole vision went red, like I was looking at an abstract painting before everything went black.

"Nicole, Nicole," a man said to me as he touched my shoulder and rocked me gently on the right side of my body.

I slowly opened my eyes. I was aware of the surgeon saying this to me. As I opened my eyes, I felt myself almost dialling back into this physical realm.

Standing all around me were these guides. There were 3 of them, all dressed in red robes. A woman was standing on my right side and holding my hand. She had long blonde flowing hair and blue eyes and was about 35 years old. She was the most beautiful woman I have ever seen in my entire life. The loving energy coming off of her made her so beautiful.

A man was holding my feet. He had shoulder-length hair, starry blue eyes, and looked like a white Jesus, with a beard and curly waves. The third presence was a man standing to my left. He was more of a larger man, with his arms out like he was holding space. He looked like a Hawaiian Kahuna. They were all in these red robes. They were all working together as a team. They looked as if they were giving me a healing and they were talking about me.

I knew they were completely invested in my recovery and improving my condition. They had held the fort the entire time and were there when I was coming out of surgery to wake me up.

I adjusted my eyes, blinking a few times. I was shocked I could receive so much information all at once without a word being said. Without even a full ten seconds to take it in. It was me dialing into this realm, waking up out of anesthetics.

I then noticed the surgeon standing over me, the nurse standing at my feet, and another nurse, who had also apparently seen me for a reading once, standing on my left. They were all making sure I was back.

I assumed they were taking me straight to recovery, and I'd be on my way in a few hours. The surgeon explained to me that my gallbladder was in a very poor acute state. He told me that he needed to keep me there overnight for observation. I lucked out and got my own room, the only one available. I was fine with that. I could see I was well taken care of. I was loved and in the right hands. I may have said some embarrassing things then, but I like to selectively forget those moments.

I daydreamed for the rest of the day, thinking about the angels that stood over me. Every time I thought of it, a wave came over me like a rush, filling me with tears. In Spiritualism, they don't use terms like angels. They refer to them as guides, spirit team or friends. They teach that angels were not like the commercialised version where they had fluffy white wings, halos over their heads and long white gowns, playing harps in the clouds, like the ones in the Philadelphia cream cheese commercials from the 90s. They are beings of light and messengers. But how I knew these were angels, I don't know. It was just a feeling. They were high-frequency.

I wondered why they were all dressed in red robes, what their assignment was with me, and how blessed I was to have them there.

My friends who knew about the surgery texted me or messaged me on Facebook. My only response, probably still a bit high from all the morphine, was, "*I am amazing! I got to meet angels in red robes! I am going to be okay.*" That's what I kept writing back, not thinking about the effects of the drugs.

Later that evening, I was left to entertain myself. During COVID, on Vancouver Island, visitors or anyone around us were prohibited in hospitals. If the nurse came in, everyone had to put their masks back on, and I was way too activated from my visit to the spiritual realm to really doze off and sleep. So, I opened my phone and hit Google. "*ANGELS IN RED ROBES*", I typed it in and hit enter. It popped up immediately. Articles and published books on the Red Ray Angels. I was shocked that this was a thing. I couldn't believe my eyes. I started opening the articles and reading as much information as I could. What I found was quite evident in my experience.

The Red Ray Angels come close to earth on Fridays. They are known as the angels who help with humanitarian work, service and ministry—helping people who follow a life of service, supporting them and keeping them on track. They were also known to help assist with healing anything related to the solar plexus - gallbladder, kidneys, digestion, colon.

I was apprenticing to be a minister. I had my surgery on Friday, and my gallbladder surgery was in my solar plexus. It was all in alignment. I don't know why I questioned before—another good reason to never take another person's word as truth. I always have my own experience and check the evidence. These angels wanted me to know they were really there and to prove to me that they had a specific reason to be. That 12 years ago, when the angel told me in the emergency room that if I stayed, I needed to do this work, not knowing at the time what this work was. It was more apparent than anything now. I was living and breathing this work. My life was a path of service. I was guided to share my experiences with those whom I could assist and help through healing and guidance. In whatever form it needed to come in.

****

Three years later. It was Matthew's birthday. We were joking about having a cake with buttercream icing. We laughed that that was what put me in the hospital three years ago around this date. We were meeting my parents for dinner in Mill Bay, BC, at the marina, and on our way, I randomly decided to stop and renew our car insurance (because it was due in a week). While there, I asked for a new license plate as ours was starting to look tattered. She reached under her desk and pulled out the next available license plate, which displayed the number 111. I looked at it briefly, wondering about the deeper meaning of all those 1s. I have seen a lot of 1s in my life before, always 1:11 or 11:11, and decided to look it up a deeper meaning of that angel number. What I found was interesting.

"The Red Ray Angels communicate with you in 111. If you see that number around you, it means they are working with you intently."

I laughed. Here I was three years later, to the date when I had my surgery, and my Red Ray Angels were still giving me a sign that they were working closely with me. Life is always better when you have Spirit along your side.

Ordination

May 23rd, 2021

The three years I trained for ministry were nothing about the books I read, the courses I took and the exams I passed at the end of it. That was easy! So was learning to do the services and writing scripts for weddings and eulogies for funerals. It was about the shifts and changes that happened internally. I went through a shift from who I felt I was to who I was being called to be from within. Any unfinished business in my life came up to look at, and anything festering under the surface got mirrored back to me in personality clashes. If I didn't think I was good enough, someone would tell me I wasn't good enough. I realised in my process that the most important aspect was that I was there to serve, be compassionate and help empower people. I could only help people with that if I were vibrating it from within my being.

The experience around my health was a huge wake-up call to being kind to myself and not putting myself last. It has been a constant check-in for finding balance in my life. The more love and kindness I give to myself, the more full I am to be able to help others. This may be why Dianne gave me the health warning before I started my training. This was a theme for mediums, that they needed to find balance within their lives and not give more than they were able to. I needed to learn and practice love and kindness in all aspects of my life. The more I do this and practice self-love, the more I feel the ripple effect and compassion for humanity.

The day came for my ordination in ministry. I decided not to wait for the world to open back up again. At this point, nobody knew when it would be. It was important to do my ordination when completing my studies instead of letting it drag on for an unknown timeframe. I felt like I was living through a revolution, and it felt pivotal in the timing of my training finishing. We did it in my friend Maureen's backyard under her tree. We used the online platform Zoom to include all who felt called to come and watch the live stream, and I said my vows to become the newest Spiritualist Minister in BC, Canada. My parents came, Matthew and my two good friends, Lana and Jewels, who helped me every step of the way through the process. Reverend Dianne Burrough and Reverend Patricia Gunn were there to ordain me. Elizabeth Menard from Two Worlds was there to represent me in my new position as a minister.

Dianne placed the stole around my neck and gave me the minister's ring. Six other spiritualist ministers had worn this specific ring before me. I was the 7th down the line to be granted this ring. It is a huge honour and privilege.

I was also gifted the omen of a white robin that flew before us and landed in front of my family and I after dinner that evening. I felt blessed to see something so rare and something none of us had ever witnessed before. Birds are amazing messengers from the spirit realm.

I have never seen my future or where ministry takes me, only the next step. Probably so I don't get ahead of myself, and so I stay present. Until then, I couldn't fully comprehend that Dianne would be retiring from spiritualist ministry within a week of my ordination, which meant I was the new solo minister at Two Worlds. Dianne had been my rock through the entire process and I will be forever grateful for her mentorship through my ministry training.

I was unsure if I was ready to step into the position when I did, but I bravely walked in anyway. I knew who walked with me in spirit and that my training would never be officially over, at least in this lifetime. The spirits walking with me in ministry are no joke! Honestly, it feels like a non-physical bodyguard team.

I often wonder how this happened and how I was mysteriously led from A to B. It was never a path I would have chosen for myself (if I picked it, I'd be living in a cabin in the woods with dogs and doing art all day), yet the calling led and guided me since I was in that church at 14. When I am giving a service, and I feel the presence of spirit pouring through me and my mouth is moving, and I am touching people's souls in the audience, I know I am in the right place, and there is nowhere in the world that I'd rather be. Opening my hands to the unknown and allowing this spiritual gift to pour through me is the most fulfilling feeling I have ever felt.

There is nothing like it. It makes everything worth it, a life bigger than me.

Chapter 12: Gratitude

~

Mission Accomplished

"What the caterpillar calls the end, the rest of the world calls a butterfly" - Lao Tzu

Spring 2023

I was attending a funeral for a friend within the community. It was on Zoom, and it was a Jewish service. Aaron was a community healer and my acupuncturist. He was in his early 40's and one of the most unique people I had ever met. He was a little man with huge energy, was health conscious, disciplined in his health, kind, generous and full of wisdom. Wherever he went, he had a huge waitlist of clients waiting to see him so he could read their energy and assist them in their health. I admired him and adored who he was, even though we weren't necessarily close. I used to see him at a time of my life when I really needed that boost.

I met him when I moved back to Vancouver Island to start my business in 2012, and he was one of the first people I met when I moved back here. I randomly met him at a cafe in Victoria, BC, with a mutual friend as they walked in. He shared that he was an acupuncturist, and I could see there was something special about him. I wanted to be a part of his healing community. He helped me see that growing my healing business was totally possible, and also it could grow when I aligned with what I truly loved. His philosophy in life was when he truly did what he loved, new clients would show up in his practice. Whether it was singing, going to concerts, community events, chi gong, or scootering around town. The more he did things he loved and enjoyed, people would find him, and they did. He also believed if he sat around pining over his business, trying to attract clients, or making people see how knowledgeable as an acupuncturist he was, his business would stagnate. I loved his philosophy, and he demonstrated it beautifully.

Aaron passed at 41 years old after having stomach cancer for the second time. He healed it the first time at 37, and the second time, he had it for nearly a year. He was realising shortly after his second diagnosis that this was going to take his life. The moment he surrendered to death and stopped fighting it, he felt peace in his heart.

I didn't understand. Why could such a beautiful human be taken from this world so young? How could someone so full of life, with so much ambition, goals, and willingness to live fully, be taken? Of course, I recognised it always seemed to be those who lived so fully that they got taken early, and maybe it was because they fulfilled what they came here to do. But with Aaron, I didn't understand why he had to die such a painful death, especially when he demonstrated health, wellness and stability on all levels of his life. If anyone could heal this, he could.

As I attended his funeral service over Zoom, I watched his family in the front row crying, sharing stories of how amazing he was and how, from birth, they called him their star being because he was born with these huge blue crystal eyes. It broke my heart to see his family in so much pain, having to let go of such an amazing human, and it felt so out of order to me.

Before the service, Matthew and I decided that after the funeral on Zoom, we would go for a drive to Cow Bay and get some sourdough bread. I woke up having a huge craving for some, and we thought that would be an excellent way to decompress after the service.

When the rabbi talked during the service, she mentioned Aaron's love for sourdough bread. It made me laugh, realising that he was already working his magic, even if he had only been gone for 48 hours. I laughed, thinking, *"Was that really my thought that I wanted sourdough? Or was that Aaron influencing me?"* Stuff like this happens often. One time, I cooked Vietnamese food for a week, and I could not get enough of it, only to have a client sit with me for a mediumship reading, and I brought through his grandmother, a Vietnamese woman who ran a restaurant. I have realised that sometimes the clients I have booked in, their loved ones in spirit visit me closer to the date, making impressions on me without me even realising it, only for it to be used as evidence in their reading.

After the service, we quietly drove to Cow Bay and went to True Grains Bakery, 40 minutes from our house. I got my bread and a snack to eat and, standing outside of the bakery holding our dog Gracie by the leash while Matthew was in there finishing up. I started to feel this swirl of energy like a vortex all around me and within me. It was like I was within a cyclone of energy which wrapped around me. I bit into my sourdough bread and started chewing it, and I heard this sound within me going, *"Mmmmmmmmm! Thank you for that. I just needed one more bite"*. The cyclone feeling suddenly spun up and out, and Aaron was standing before me. I was back to my normal self, but he was staring right at me. I spoke to him telepathically, saying, *"Why, why did you have to die? Couldn't you beat this? Couldn't you have healed yourself like you helped so many other people heal? We needed you!"*

Aaron smiled. He looked right at me in his eyes with his starry blue eyes and winked. *"Mission accomplished."* Then, he was gone in a flash.

"Mission accomplished," I thought. Huh, okay then. He really was done. I took a deep breath and sighed. At that moment, I accepted it, but it didn't stop being sad.

As the days passed, I noticed that that word was used more than once. I finished a painting of a bear I had done, and one of my medium friends, Jewels, wrote to me, *"Mission accomplished"*. I wondered if she realised what she had said. But it made me laugh that now I had heard it twice that day.

Four months later, I was at the Arthur Findlay College of Psychic Science in Stansted, England, and Aaron came through in one of the student demonstrations on the platform in the sanctuary.

He came and presented himself as a friend in spirit. A little man who drove a scooter, was larger than life, a healer and had a glorious death, which Aaron did. After eight months of dying of cancer, he made the conscious decision to do MAID. He had ten friends and family around him, and they all held space and chanted with him as he passed away. According to his friends and family, at the funeral, it was the most beautiful ceremony. The fact that the medium picked up on it was significant to me—a glorious death. To me, that was another validation that doing MAID was not wrong. In fact, for Aaron, it was mind-blowingly sexy and amazing, so much so that he made the effort all the way from spirit to report back to let us know that it was so. When she got to the message of the reading, she said, *"Just one more time, he wants you to know that it's not sad that he died, but his mission was accomplished."*

Perfect, I thought. Just like that, the healing energy moved through me, the power of this work brought to me such peace. A few words could put this to rest once and for all. I was so grateful for that. When a loved one dies who was so full of life, and you have a hard time making peace with it, remember- their mission was accomplished.

Mediumship ~ It's Not About Death, But Life

"I then understood that even if my physical body stopped, everything is still perfect in the greater tapestry of life, for we never truly die."
- Anita Moorjani

Over the years of being a medium, I have been asked by many friends, family and acquaintances if the work I do is heavy or depressing. Yes, sometimes it is, but it's incredibly meaningful, light and soulful most of the time. I feel blessed to do what I do, and, most importantly, mediumship has taught me more about living life. It has removed my fear of the unknown of leaving this world, as any faith or belief has turned into knowing. I know without a doubt that there is an afterlife, and when I die from my physical body, I will continue my existence on another plane in spirit form. Spirit has proved that enough to me with evidence.

Blending my energy with loved ones in spirit has allowed me the ability to learn from people's living experiences what they did well, what they failed at, who they loved, what they enjoyed and what they could have done better. I have learned so much from spirits about appreciating the little things, the importance of forgiveness, taking responsibility, and making the most out of the ordinary.

Spirit has taught me about the beauty of Mother Earth. Yes, we come here to experience human emotions; things get intense, and our lives can change in an instant, but it is one of the reasons we chose to come to Earth, to feel things fully and experience contrast. We picked our parents and experiences we chose to have and learn from. As difficult as it is to understand at times when we are on our hands and knees begging for mercy, pain is one way we can learn to let go and grow to new heights.

Life is so much of what you make it. I have done readings for cynics, and what you say doesn't matter. It is never good enough. The way some people view the world can be so closed off. You could be handing them life's greatest blessing on a plate, and they'd still think it was dirt. I have read for people who are so open to life's opportunity, allowance of synchronicity, and choose to see the good in people. I see how we all may live in the same world but can have a completely different experience of it. You get to choose what is worth living for. You are here to find what makes you come to life. You are meant to follow the flow of energy that brings joy into your world. It's important to find soul expressions and not to take this world too seriously. It's all just a cosmic joke, anyway! At least, that's what I tell myself.

Most importantly, you realise that we cannot die, and we take ourselves with us wherever we go. Things don't really go away, as energy cannot be created or destroyed. We are all woven into this tapestry of life together. Although we cannot change people, we can change ourselves. And in that, our feelings and thoughts towards another may change if we give it the opportunity to.

Life will give you what you need to learn, and every opportunity that comes to you is a chance to turn things around. If I hadn't lost so many loved ones in the first 20 years of my life, I would have never even thought of walking down the path as a medium. I would have had no use for it. However, my reoccurring meetings with death forced me to see life through another lens, or I would have drowned in the depression. I needed to get curious and understand more, as I couldn't accept that life was just all suffering. And because of that, I felt I had been given the greatest gift. Not a belief but a knowing of life after death, that life continues, far, far beyond this Earth plane, and I will see my loved ones again...

Saying Goodbye

September 2023

    I was on my way home from hospice, as one of my dear friends and long-term clients, who I met from the Cowichan Spiritualist Church 8 years prior, had been suffering from cancer and had decided to have a Medical Assisted Death. She had asked me to be there with her for her event, alongside a few of her family members and a couple of close friends.

As I was driving home, I reflected on my day and thought about the beauty I witnessed in her transition. I could only wish everyone to have a gentle death like Pamela did. Her faith and Spirituality greatly helped in her transition. She looked so peaceful and was so sure of where she was going and was already having visitations from family members in spirit. The lights were dimmed, her favourite music was playing in the background, and she was with her family and close friends wrapped around her. I said a prayer with everyone there, calling in all her support from Spirit and asked for a graceful transition and celebration on her reunion home.

I tell each loved one when they pass away to call me when you get there. I say this under my breath and then let go, knowing they will reach me however they choose when they are ready and without expectations. I often look forward to their creativity in how they will reach me in unexpected ways. All I know is when I let go, I am always met in awe when I least expect it.

When I got home that evening from my drive and highly emotional day, I decided to decompress by sitting in the dark in a quiet meditation and honour Pamela. I needed to empty my thoughts and settle my revved-up nervous system as there was such a rollercoaster of emotions letting her go. Not to mention, I had to officiate a wedding the next day and needed to be ready for that. Before closing my eyes, I took a moment to appreciate Pamela for our friendship and her influence on my life, for all that she was and who she was to me. I then let my mind empty and dropped into my meditation with a deep breath. Before I could completely let go and close my eyes, this song popped into my head out of nowhere and repeated loudly to take my focus away. It was a song I hadn't heard or even thought of in probably 20 years. It was *I'm Already There* by Lonestar.

It was blaring in my ears, and I couldn't think about anything else. The lyrics played in my head repeatedly as I tried to close my eyes…

> *"I'm already there,*
> *Take a look around,*
> *I'm the sunshine in your hair,*
> *I'm the shadow in the ground.*
> *I'm the whisper in the wind,*

And I'll be there till the end,
As I know, I am in your prayers,
I'm already there."

I grabbed my phone, downloaded the song to my Apple Music, and listened immediately. Even though the song may have different meanings, it was the chorus I heard. It was relevant, and it was exactly Pamela's experience. She didn't go anywhere, she didn't leave. She was right here. Humour followed me as I laughed at the thought that I always asked my loved ones to call me when they got there. She was right there with me, and no time had been needed between her passing and showing up for me. Of course, I thought, all our loved ones in spirit are already there. Just take a look around-they are the sunshine in our hair, they are the shadows in the ground, they are the whispers in the wind, and they will be with us till the end. They will always be in your prayers, as they are already there with you.

Your loved ones in spirit are not far, even when it feels this way. They have never left and are not lost, nor do they need to be found. They are right here with you in your heart. They are in your presence and a part of you as you grow. There is nowhere to get to in order to reach them, as they are only just a thought away. As you learn to empty your mind and surrender to love, you will realise all you have been searching for is right here. The greatest gift you can give yourself is to discipline your mind and nurture that love connection through your heart. It's a fast track to Spirit. That is how you open up so you are reachable. There is no trick to love, and it is available to all of us. You can connect to any loved one in this world or another by the love you share. That feeling in your heart cannot be erased, just remembered and is timeless.

Pamela reminded me in her passing that we cannot be divided, as you cannot separate from the whole. You do have free will and can choose to see things from other perspectives. Our world can look lonely, isolated, and divided in that perception. But when you turn back to love and into that remembrance of the love you shared, you will realise they didn't go anywhere, and there is nowhere to get to. It's just a shift in awareness back to love and that they are already there.

Heaven On Earth

"I slept and dreamt that life was joy. I awoke and saw that life was service. I acted and behold, service was joy." -
Rabindranath Tagore

I was sitting at the local pub restaurant with a couple of my soul friends. We were sharing conversation over nachos while looking out at Lake Cowichan with the sun beaming onto our faces on an early summer afternoon. We talked about what we were all up to that summer, what was calling us from within and where we were being guided to share our work in the near future.

Craig asked me, *"So, Nicole, with all the work you've been doing for years with people in private practice, communicating with deceased loved ones, reading people, what do you think the meaning of life really is?"*

"Joy," I said, smiling.

"Really? You think that's it?"

"Yes, absolutely", I answered as I drank my soda water and absorbed the sunlight.

Craig then shared a story about when he was a young boy and slipped, hitting his head and going unconscious. He talked about how he went to this place of absolute pure bliss. It was a state of being so peaceful and loving that he never wanted it to end. He shared that his parents splashed cold water on his face and shook him to bring him back, but he didn't want to leave that blissful state. *"Why, if Heaven or the afterlife is a place of pure joy and bliss, would I want to come here? Why would I come here to experience joy if I have it there?"*

"Because we have it in Heaven, but our purpose is to bring that bliss and joy into our everyday life here. To bring Heaven to Earth. It's to find joy in absolutely everything. Not to mention that life does get better when we choose to live a path of joy. No longer do you live life like you are missing out. No more feeling like you are in this hustle and grind. You relax into life, and you start to appreciate each moment."

We all took in what was being said. Darlene shared that that was very much her philosophy of life, too. It kept her from feeling like she needed to be doing more so that she could spend more time in the moment with herself and others.

I used to think I came to this Earth with this great mission. I had to pledge my way through with hustle and grind to get somewhere. Unconsciously, some of me thought I had to work my way into Heaven as if I needed to accomplish something to get back there. But I was looking at it as outside accomplishments. I needed to prove my worth and make it…whatever the heck that meant.

In May 2018, when I did my first Ayahuasca ceremony with an indigenous shaman, the teachings came to me clear as day. There really was nowhere to get to. Life was about living in joy, being as present as I could in each moment, doing things that brought me happiness in life, and choosing to really live. If I focused on incorporating joy into my life and did things that brought me bliss, I would live an incredibly fulfilling life. But I was not here to prove anything to anyone but to live fully in my authentic self. That alone would create a positive ripple and help raise the vibration of the planet, and that was my meaning here.

Now, I can't speak to everyone, but I can speak to those who may feel a resonance in the words that I have written. If you are hustling, grinding, working yourself to the ground, putting your work life ahead of your quality of life and your work ahead of your health, you may be missing what life is trying to teach you.

Also, there is more to this life than constantly learning lessons. Yes, you are here to learn, but you do not need to be in a never-ending cycle of healing, spinning your wheels, trying to learn lessons from each person you meet. I have seen more people hurt themselves by toxic and abusive situations than simply stepping out of it. It is in stepping out of it that perspective is received, and usually, it's then that the teaching comes, not when you are in a constant merry-go-round with an unhealthy dynamic.

Life is simple: to love, forgive easily, learn from your life experiences, share your gifts, do things that bring you joy and make the most of the journey you are on. You are not all given the same opportunities in life, but you have things you have chosen to look at and grow from. You may find more peace and bliss in this lifetime when you choose to learn and grow from a path of joy. It doesn't always have to be hard. The more you say life is hard, the harder it will get, as your thoughts create a vibration, and your vibration is what creates your outcome.

But Heaven is right here. It is not out there. It's a state of mind and a place in consciousness. Why else do your loved ones in spirit say, *"I am right here with you"* Or *"I am forever in your heart."* To understand this concept is to realise that that place you long for, home, is right here, in your heart. You have to tune into it and you can create that by bringing it into your stillness and meditation. To feel at home in your heart. Most importantly, know that being in your joy is the greatest gift you have to offer this world.

Heaven never went anywhere. It's right here in the trees, the ocean, the river, the sun, and the moon. When you are on the other side, you are simply a part of all creation. You are part of the infinite power, the intelligence that creates the whole, and you are exactly where you need to be. You are home.

Initiation

"You've always had the power my dear, you just had to learn it for yourself." - Glinda the Good Witch, *Wizard of Oz* quote from Frank L. Baum

September 2023

On a silent retreat, I was in Sedona, Arizona, learning from one of my most precious spiritual teachers, Lola Jones from Divine Openings. Her book had fallen into my lap right around the time I got ordained as a Spiritualist minister in 2021. The year prior, I had had difficult contact with a spiritual teacher/shaman just a few weeks before the pandemic and lockdown started. This shaman had given me feedback on who she felt I was and how she saw me, but her style of feedback felt unjust and I fell deep into shame, and I had a hard time shaking it. I didn't feel seen or heard for who I was, just what she assessed about me. I couldn't stand it when people put me in a box of who they felt I was.

Shortly after, I ended up having my gallbladder out, which I believe had a lot to do with doing the ketogenic diet long term, mixed with the emotional pain I was dealing with, as well as the turmoil going on in the world. I was hanging on by a string, attempting to pull myself back together. Even though I decided against her feedback, I could still hear her voice in the back of my head telling me I wasn't good enough and to shut down my business as I was taking people's power away. She told me I was a performer, not a spiritual teacher, and that I didn't have reverence or respect for true spiritual work.

She was from another part of the world, and her teachings and way of life were very different, especially in their spiritual work. I wanted to like her. I wanted her to like me, and I wanted to be seen for who I was. But it felt like the more I tried, the worse it got. I can see it now for what it was- just a mismatch in energy.

At that time, I was looking for help to regain my confidence, someone to guide me on the next phase of my evolving journey. I was exhausted, yet I was searching as I wanted to do this work with reverence and integrity. In order to share this work with others, I felt I needed someone with more experience than me in the subject to learn from, be of service to, and share what I had to offer. This is a way for me to never stop growing and to have the opportunity to go beyond my limited senses.

Lola came to me and offered me a new path of grace. She saw in me what I shunned in myself and gave that power back to me. Working with her, I was instantly re-filled with life force energy, vitality and trust in myself. She reminded me that there was an easier way to walk through life other than constantly being in self-assessment. Pulling myself to pieces wasn't helpful, and I didn't need to do rigorous spiritual teachings to awaken. Grace could do the heavy lifting in my life, and I held the power. She reminded me to see my good qualities, embody love and be clear about who I was.

In Sedona, we were at Buddha Beach, a feminine energy vortex at the bottom of Cathedral Rock. We walked far into the trail, where we found a creek, peaceful and quiet. We swam in the cool, crisp water and sunbathed on this giant rock. There were 8 of us, and we all found a place to lay on this warm, sun-heated rock. It was glorious. It was the end of the retreat, and Lola, usually on the last evening, would do an eye initiation for us to guide us back to ourselves.

When she gazed into my eyes at first, I felt nothing. Maybe it was a little awkward as I locked eyes and didn't move them. However, a few minutes into it, she held my hands and closed her eyes. I followed, and as I did that, I felt this energy transference return to me. I heard the word *"teacher"* melt into my heart. As I welcomed those parts of me that were lost, I reclaimed them fully. I felt the gift of my spirit come back to me in ways I didn't know I needed to. Tears rolled down my face as I felt my power return to me times ten. The power that I lost and gave to that shaman who saw me in another light. The words that told me I shouldn't, nor was I worthy of the path I was on. The words that took from me that I didn't want to give power to anymore.

Even though I had been doing this work for most of my adult life, going deeper into service and deeper into the state of love that called to move through me, I never fully claimed what I did nor saw my worth in it. I could never really see or fully understand why I was busy with the work I did. I couldn't see my own worth in it, and I felt that, as long as I stayed focused on service and doing this work for something bigger, I would be guided where to go. The more I did that, the more it worked.

But that day, something changed. I started to feel my worth in what I offered the world. The power within me was more than just service to give. Divine love was filling me in so many ways that I could not even comprehend it. The gifts were an endless expansion. I would never let somebody tell me who I was again or dictate my worth. At that moment, I saw myself as a divine expression worthy of all the love the creator had to give me. I was here to share my gifts with the world and let in and fully embrace the love of the divine. For the first time, I really saw myself how Spirit saw me through their loving eyes. After this eye initiation, I laid down on my back and opened my arms. I claimed it and basked in the glory. I let in all the love.

"No more", I whispered to myself. *"No more would I ever let anyone tell me who I was or what I was capable of. That was between me and the divine. That was our agreement and not to give to anyone else."* I felt the pain melt away from me. I felt the burden I had carried in my stomach leave my body and melt into the rock. Compassion and forgiveness filled me as I set myself free. I had expanded, and I was more ready to share my gifts with the world and help people see that power within themselves and know their worth, too.

The spiritual journey is filled with opportunities, trials and tribulations to find your worth and reclaim your power. The people in your life play will show up and show you where you are and where you are not owning your worth or gifts within you. Your path will look like no one else's, and you will have your own roadmap to walk down. What will be significant for one person will not be for another, but whatever your theme in your journey in life, know that with more love for self and connection to Spirit, you can grow through anything. You will always grow and expand with your connection to the infinite. You will never arrive as you will always be expanding and will always have the opportunity to overcome things you felt at the time were impossible. Never let anyone tell you who you are or what you are capable of. Choose people in your life who see your value and worth, not ones to whom you have to prove yourself. Life requires willingness, focus and intention to overcome any obstacle. If you are brave enough to step forward and dream beyond your wildest imagination, the steps in front will guide you. The power of love will lead you and change the shape and course of your life. It was never about becoming anything but remembering who you truly are.

May you allow your heart to always lead and guide you to love and grace.

Appendix

~

7 Principles of Spiritualism

I am a Reverend in the faith of Spiritualism, and I wanted to start by sharing the 7 principles that Spiritualists follow as a philosophy and way of life. These are principles, not commandments, and include no dogma or creed. They are to contemplate and incorporate into your everyday living. Spiritualism is a religion, philosophy and science. These principles have been updated by Two Worlds Spiritualist Centre in Nanaimo, BC, Canada, where I am the resident minister. They are updated to reflect our current norms and modern language.

The 7 Principles of Spiritualism are based upon a belief in:

1. The Existence of a Divine Creator

2. The Creation of the Divine Family of Humanity

3. Communications, Guidance and Healing from Spirit

4. Continuous Existence of the Soul

5. Personal Responsibility

6. The Existence of the Spiritual Law of Cause and Effect

7. Eternal Progress open to all Souls

The concepts and original wording, updated above, came through the Mediumship of Emma Hardinge Britten as she communicated with the spirit of Robert Owen in 1871. She was a Spiritualist Medium and a great speaker on the philosophy of Spiritualism. Below are the original 7 principles.

The Original 7 Principles are:

1. The Fatherhood of God

2. The Brotherhood of Man

3. The Communion of Spirits and the Ministry of Angels

4. The Continuous Existence of the Human Soul

5. Personal Responsibility

6. Compensation and Retribution Hereafter for the Good and Evil Deeds done on Earth

7. Eternal Progress open to every Human Soul

Dictionary

Angels: Spirit beings of a very high frequency. In Spiritualism, they can be also be considered your loved ones in spirit or guides who walk amongst you.

Arthur Findlay College: A Spiritualist College in Stansted, UK, where mediums come from all over the world to study.

Aura: The energy field around the body.

Blending: Blending energies with a spirit.

Circle: A mediumship development circle for unfolding your mediumship.

Evidential mediumship: Bringing through relevant information that is validated from the client who is receiving the reading.

In Spirit: Someone who has passed away.

Linking in: Shifting your awareness into spirit and letting a spirit come to you.

Shaman: A medicine person who is a bridge between worlds, communing with the spirit world and physical world with the main focus on healing.

Smudging: A sacred tradition that involves burning herbs with prayer and intention to purify and cleanse your auric field and the space you are cleansing.

Tuning In: When the medium shifts their awareness to read the situation. They may tune into a person or tune into a spirit.

Acknowledgements

First off, I'd like to thank my husband, Matthew Ashdown, for enhancing this book and making it even better than I could ever do for myself.

For Katie Omen, my book coach and editor, this book would not have happened without your guidance; trust me, I tried twice over seven years. Your consistency, professional opinion, belief in me and coaching made a world of difference.

For my parents and family for giving me a good upbringing and a positive self-image. The older I get, the more I appreciate it.

I'd like to thank all my loved ones in spirit; I felt your holy presence through the writing of this book, and even just mentioning you gives me goosebumps: Steve, Mary, Crista, Grandparents on my mom's side ~ Nana and Papi, and grandparents on my dad's side ~ Nana and Papi. Also my newer friends in spirit: Jewleana, Aaron and Pamela. And let's not forget my mini poodle, Ebony, for forever being in my heart.

To my guides and the ones I acquired while writing this book. Thank you for helping me remember anything is possible and can be elevated when I include you in what I am doing.

I'd like to thank my spiritual teachers who have guided me and led me on this path. The ones that taught me energy healing, meditation, card readings, tarot, shamanism, fieldwork, mediumship, spiritualism, ministry, coaching, business training, consciousness and evolution. Not only the amazingly good ones filled with integrity that I look up to but also the ones that weren't so great and caused me to question. Thank you for all the teachable moments so I know what to do and what not to do when I teach my students. I am forever grateful for your presence on my journey.

I'd like to thank my awesome friends for walking this path with me and making life way more interesting and fun. I love that we can support each other and continue to grow. I have way more friends than I can name here, but please know that your presence means the world to me.

My photographer Brandy-Lee Planiden for taking awesome pictures for this book! You are the best photographer.

To our team at Two Worlds Spiritualist Centre for your support and trust in me as your minister as we run our amazing centre together.

To all my mediumship circle students, you keep me inspired and innovative with your weekly presence and curiosity. Thank you for being loving and supportive of each other.

There are so many great memories, the magic we have created together is miracles in action.

To my private practice clients, thank you so much for trusting me and allowing me to be a conduit of spirit for you. Being of service this way has been the greatest gift anyone could ask for.

For all my medium friends and colleagues, know that I see you and admire you for all the service you put in the world. Thank you for raising the bar and inspiration.

Thank you to all the cool people out there who are sharing their gifts to the world, it's your positive ripple that makes this world a better place!

To technology, for creating Grammarly, Scrivener, Zoom, iPhones and MacBooks, I have to acknowledge you because you made my life easier as a writer! I can't imagine writing this book on a typewriter and wasting so much paper on endless drafts.

And thank you to Mother Earth. I am so grateful for my opportunity to live on this planet at this time in humanity.

Thank you, Thank you, Thank you.

About The Author

Nicole Powell is a Spiritual Medium and Reverend in Lake Cowichan, BC, on Vancouver Island. She works in her community and online, leading spiritualist services, readings, running circles and leading workshops. She is the minister at Two Worlds Spiritualist Centre in Nanaimo, Vancouver Island.

Nicole loves walking through the forest, listening to audios and music that keep her inspired. She lives close to the river where she spends a lot of time. She has a wonderful husband Matthew Ashdown and a sweet mini doodle named Gracie. In Nicole's free time, she enjoys travelling the world and exploring sacred sites, sitting at home painting until the late hours of the evening, and writing what catches her inspiration. Together, their life is simple, creative and peaceful. They live with great meaning and purpose in as much as they can. This is Nicole's first book, and she feels there is so much more to come…

Visits Nicole's website @
www.nicolepowell.ca

If you enjoyed this book, please post a review on Amazon so others may find it to read. Thank you!

Printed in Great Britain
by Amazon